# SOLO

A GUIDE TO BOARDGAMES FOR THOSE WITHOUT FRIENDS

# Paul Oyston

Book Cover by Shelly Oyston

First edition March 2023

For information contact :
oystonwrites@gmail.com

ISBN: 978-1-7393263-0-2

# Introduction

Growing up in the 80's most families had the usual selection of classic board games, Monopoly, Trivial Pursuit and a copy of Operation that never had batteries in it. Countless rainy afternoons would be spent playing The Game of Life or carefully constructing the Mouse Trap that would inevitably fail at the point where the small plastic diving man was supposed to unleash the cage on the unsuspecting rodent below.

I never felt a true love for board games growing up, the rise of the personal computer and games consoles drew me away from games of Monopoly with cheating relatives. Instead I settled into a land of Super Mario, The Legend of Zelda and an ever expanding roster of Nintendo games that would continue to hold my affection to this day.

Cardboard tokens and dice just couldn't hold a flame to a controller and a rapidly expanding television screen, why spend your afternoon playing Cluedo when you could watch The Terminator?

I fell back into board games in my early teens, moving into fantasy territory with Blood Bowl and the Alien inspired Space Hulk that a kid from school owned. Unfortunately it became increasingly difficult finding friends with the same interests (It was all about grunge and girls at this point). Board games took a back seat to the Playstation and Xbox.

And that's how it stayed, for a long time.

Fast forward a couple of decades. Marriage, kids, full time employment and the sense of 'been there, done that' with gaming led to the first signs of a new obsession to appear.

It started with party games, Exploding Kittens and Cards Against Humanity, the 'hilarious', and now admittedly fairly problematic, fill in the blanks card game. Then Jackbox, a digital party game on PC and console where anyone could join in as long as they had a phone or a tablet. At the time it was a revelation that these experiences could turn a few drinks with a couple of friends into a fun, if a little raucous night where everyone was left eager to get together and play again.

In my search for more, I found that a rich world of board games had sprung up in my absence. From social deduction games to dungeon crawlers. From dexterity games to resource management games that require a full day to play, the wealth of experiences on offer was mind boggling.

Now, as an adult, armed with a small amount of disposable income and just enough spare time on my hands, I was ready to dive head first into this new exciting world. The only thing missing was people to play with.

Party games were fine, you could pull out an inflatable man and play charades with him, everyone was up for that. A few rounds of exploding kittens or shouting about crabs definitely filled an evening but I wanted more. I had found this treasure trove of experiences but finding people to sit down and learn new games was difficult.

Get new friends you say, believe me I've tried but it was hard enough finding this lot. And let's be real here, just because I found this whole thing new and exciting didn't mean they had to. Nobody wants to be the guy ruining everyone's fun, trying to explain the rules to overly complicated games when all they want to do is shout 'CRABS' at you until you lose the will to live.

I found that there was only one answer.

Solo Gaming!

# What do you mean, solo gaming?

Solo board gaming can come in many different forms and this book will take you through some of the many ways you can enjoy it. The first thing to establish is what solo board gaming isn't. It's not a person taking multiple turns of imaginary people round the table, landing on your imaginary opponents' Mayfair that just so  happens to have a hotel on it. Solo gaming is generally reserved for games that aren't really that competitive, however there are, of course, plenty of exceptions that we will come to later.

Solo experiences can differ from genre to genre and as hobbyist modern board games have become more popular, solo variants of games are quickly becoming key selling points. And it makes sense for creators to continue to provide these experiences as it becomes more difficult to find ways to simply relax and enjoy yourself without a screen.

The history of solo play can be traced back to the invention of Solitaire, or Patience. Thought to have been invented in the late 18th century when an imprisoned nobleman waiting for his execution during the French revolution was left to pass the time with nothing but a deck of cards. Legend has it that the game spread amongst his fellow prisoners and soon on to the aristocracy who, seemingly all had decks of cards to mess around with and plenty of spare time to do so (The Terminator wouldn't be out for a couple hundred years after all).Solitaire games spread throughout Europe, even illustrious figures such as Napoleon and Prince Albert all reportedly became avid players. Eventually it found its way onto Windows 3.0, enjoying increasing popularity on coffee breaks in offices during the 90's. Today, Solitaire games are mainly played on mobile phones or re skinned and shuffled into different genres such as Tetris, Candy Crush or Coin Frenzy and, on that note, here is a little secret for you:

If you are playing these games on your phone then you are already solo gaming!

In the world of board gaming, more and more titles are being released with solo variants in mind and even if they aren't baked into the core game itself there are vast resources available where people have 'home brewed' solo variations. These can just be slight tweaks of rules or PDF's. Sometimes custom made cards that can be printed off or to take it further, some clever boffins have even created apps that can simulate additional players or randomly generated game events!

Now some people may attach a stigma to solo board gaming, tell you it's sad, that you must feel lonely. If you feel this way it may be worth asking yourself how much time you spend watching television on your own, or how many times you've sat down to watch a movie with a nice cup of tea and some biscuits without any one else. Or even think about the hours spent playing Mario Kart with nobody else to talk to but the dog.

The truth is, Solo board gaming can be just as exciting and filled with as many standout memorable moments as playing with a group, in fact, in some ways it's better than playing with friends for the following reasons:

## No Arguments

Simply put, you're not going to spend the entire game having your game scuppered by a spiteful player who just doesn't want you to win. There is also less chance of ruining the evening and causing an atmosphere if someone is a bad loser if you are playing against the game. Although there are no guarantees that you won't want to launch it out of the window if you lose. Which brings me on to.

## More Challenging

In my experience, solo gaming can be tougher than your usual cooperative or competitive game with some brutal spikes in difficulty that help create a greater feeling of accomplishment if successful. But, if you prefer a more casual experience....

### Greater Flexibility

You can feel free to take the pressure off when going solo, ultimately it's about fun and if a game isn't doing it for you then there's nothing wrong with adjusting rules to make it more accessible. Most solo games are fairly short so it's not too much hassle to bin off a session and start again. There are some longer games though and we'll come to them soon.

### You're Always Playing

There is no 'elimination' in a solo game so you won't ever be sitting watching others finish off the game or waiting for them to take their turn. This doesn't mean that you can't lose a solo game, but if you do then that's it, you can start again.

### It's Your Game

Sometimes the worst part about playing with other players is the players themselves. Most people I have played with have been generally nice, chilled people who just want to have a bit of competitive fun but there are times when fellow players can become impatient or even annoyed if someone may be slow taking their turn or asking questions with regards to rules. There are also times when you may quickly catch a mistake you have just made and request you retake your turn, much to the annoyance of some of the more pedantic players. Solo gaming can take away the unneeded stress of having to deal with less flexible players. And if you are one of 'those people' then solo gaming can take away the unneeded stress of having to deal with slow, indecisive people.

## Less Time Teaching

If you are anything like me and have a partner who hates being told the rules of a new game then solo play is a godsend. Rather than having to bumble your way through explaining scenarios and ultimately forgetting vital parts of the game, you only have yourself to worry about. A quick look through the rules, a run through of a Youtube video walkthrough and you are away.

## An Excellent Way To Learn

Now if you are lucky enough to have someone who would love to share your passion for boardgaming, playing solo can be the perfect way to learn new titles before bringing them to the table for game night. I'm going to confess that I told a little white lie earlier when I said that solo gaming is not one person taking multiple people's turns. Sometimes, when buying a new game that may be a little more complex, I do play a few sessions alone just so that, when it comes to teaching it, I am more confident. As a result, when the time comes that you finally convince someone to play with you, all of the solo sessions you have played will help them get into the game quicker.

## Expand Your Horizons

Solo gaming has allowed me to explore games I wouldn't have looked at if I was concerned with finding a group to play with and with a bunch of smaller box games coming in at a considerably lower price than some bigger offerings, the risk is minimal.

In the end, these plus points can't fully replicate the feeling of getting a bunch of people around a table to play together but sometimes that's not what you want, sometimes it's not possible to coordinate everything just right so that you the right amount of people who all want to play the same thing at the same time. It certainly can be difficult to convince people to learn new games, nobody wants to have to read a full on powerpoint presentation after a few beers when they can just play something they already know.

# Tell me about these board games

So we are all ready to embark on a solo journey around the wonderful world of boardgames! But before we set off there are a few terms that I will use that may seem unfamiliar to you. For those that eat, sleep and drink tabletop, these terms are likely to be part of your vocabulary already so you are free to skip to chapter 3 if you want to save some time for actual playing. Be warned though, there may be some very spicy humour here you risk missing out on.

For those who stuck around! Here are a few quick explanations to get you up to speed.

## Meeple

A Meeple is your figure on the game board. A portmanteau derived from 'my people' and first used to describe the figures in the game,

Carcassonne. Traditionally they look like stout little dudes with stubby arms and are generally made from wood. They can come in various shapes and sizes from human(ish) to animal, rumour has it you can even have vegetable shaped meeples but you didn't hear that from me. Meeples are fun to hold, fun to move and it's a fun word to say too.

## Crunchy

Ooof it's crunchy!

It's likely you have already heard of the adjective 'crunchy' but when it comes to tabletop games, crunch can refer to the difficulty of the mechanics of a game, particularly when they are slightly long winded or complicated. If a game has a lot of moving parts or interlocking elements that bounce off each other then it's crunchy. If you need to roll three fistfuls of dice to open a door and then balance a year worth of VAT receipts to see if the door is creaky and wakes up a slumbering dragon then it's crunchy. If you then have to recollect the first three breakfasts you had in March 2013 then it's…. You get the idea.

Crunch can be overwhelming at times but it can add depth and systems to a game that elevates it to the kind of experience that can literally make you mutter 'oooh it's crunchy' (trust me i've done it).

It can also come in different forms, from literal number crunching to handfuls of…...bits, plastic bits, cardboard bits, wooden bits. Some of it is unnecessary but most of it oh so satisfying to chew through.

So don't be too scared if I describe something as crunchy, unless you have lots of fillings. In which case maybe stick to soft fruits and vegetables, maybe some soups.

## Gateway Game

Gateway games create new board gamers. They are considered to be suitable for someone fairly new to modern board gaming who may then move on to more complex titles.

The rules are generally simpler and implement a lot of the time themes and systems from more classic or mainstream games along with a few more complex mechanics to ease you in slowly. Don't worry though, soon you will tear off the stabilisers and pedal downhill no handed.

A lot of the games in this book could be classed as gateway games but don't let the term fool you. These games may come with a more accessible strategy but there can be plenty of depth in some of these bad boys.

## Player Board

A player board differs from a main game board that sits in the middle of your table in that each player has their own individual board placed in front of them, serving a variety of purposes.

Some games are played almost entirely on a player board, where players place tokens or Meeple, keep track of points and in some cases add modular parts to their boards to expand them. Some are integrated into game play in conjunction with the main board itself, providing quick rule references to the player, tracking individual progress or holding resources.

Having a decent player board can be like sitting behind the wheel of a spaceship (if spaceships had wheels). You have a little console in front of you with buttons and flashy pictures of stuff. Functional yet fun.

## Asymmetric

Most board games have each player starting in the same way, each with the same goals and with everyone following pretty much the same actions. In Monopoly you are a shoe or a scotty dog, throwing dice and moving round the board raking in the cash, everyone does the same thing for hours until everyone falls asleep or has a massive argument and tips the table over.

In asymmetrical games, players often start with different resources or methods of achieving their goals which aren't necessarily the same. As an example, an asymmetrical game such as Fury of Dracula has one player taking control of the infamous Vampire, using their supernatural powers to evade capture by the rest of the players who themselves control bounty hunters in a game of cat and mouse. Each set of players' goals and systems in asymmetrical games link together to make them incredibly satisfying to play as you often just have to concentrate on doing your own thing well, in order to come out on top.

## House Rules

House rules are unofficial variations to the rules of a game that can occur for plenty of different reasons. Sometimes an aspect of a game can be too difficult to get to grips with, maybe you are introducing it to a younger child or less experienced player. Sometimes you've played a game so much that someone has figured out the perfect way to win every time so you change certain rules to make it more open. Often a rule just isn't fun, or as I like to call it, utter bullsh*t, so you change a rule to prevent the game being needlessly long or frustrating.

Very often, house rules happen accidentally. If a rule has been misunderstood at the time you were learning the game then you could go on playing forever without knowing you weren't following the official rules. Monopoly is a great example of this, no two families ever play it the same way.

Should you use house rules? Of course, if it makes the game fun then house rules are perfectly fine and sometimes necessary. Sometimes, if a session is starting to become stale, then you can chuck in a last minute house rule to keep things chugging along nicely or end it early if things look like they might get a bit stale.

## Abstract Games

Abstract is a term used to categorise a game that has no theme or randomisation such as dice. Examples of abstract games could be Chess, Checkers or Go. There are numerous, modern, board games that can be considered abstract although not all of them fit every single aspect of the definition. For the purposes of this book I will mostly be using the term to describe a game with no real theme or one where the theme is so loose to be considered unimportant.

# So how can I play a board game on my own?

Dedicated solo options are becoming more common in modern hobbyist games and as such a lot of titles that are considered competitive come with an included Automa mode. An Automa is as it sounds, an automated opponent that you have the opportunity to beat, not just by scoring higher than a predetermined set total of points, but through the flow of the game itself that can throw up situations where the opponents performance will alter from game to game.

This witchcraft can be achieved by a random rolling of dice to dictate an action that the Automa takes or a dedicated deck of cards that is randomly drawn from to simulate their actions. Just think of an Automa as a sneaky robot opponent who has been magically transformed into some bits of card or a few pages of a rulebook and you won't go far wrong.

Generally, the role of an Automa is to disrupt the solo players' game as little as possible. You will generally find an Automa does little to directly mess with your plan and because this is not an A.I that is influenced by your choices, this mode tends to play itself to a certain degree. The benefit is that there is little upkeep required by you, the player meaning you are free to concentrate on your own fun rather than playing for two people.

One key advantage of an Automata is that, for the most part, the player's experience in playing the game is almost identical to playing multiplayer. Once you get past the initial learning curve of operating the Automa they can offer a really smooth playing experience and with most Automas offering a sliding scale of difficulty, you can get plenty of life out of them.

As a rule of thumb, most Cooperative games, where the goal is to beat the game rather than each other, can usually be played solo. This can be achieved in a number of ways, the first option is the fully solo route that pits one 'player' against the game. If you face a ferocious troll it's not a problem, just roll a few dice. Evil cultists? flip a card and see what you get. A lot of the time, co-op games can scale the difficulty or change some of its mechanics for what is called 'true' solo play.

The alternative is for you to play as two players, effectively cooperating with yourself. Gone are the arguments over whether you should open the door, move further around the board or roll that extra dice in the hope of a favourable outcome. Now the responsibility sits on your shoulders alone, what could go wrong? In a lot of cases, this method is the best way to experience the full game as it was intended, with fewer examples of missing mechanics or concessions made in adapting the game for one player.

On the rare occasion when a cooperative games' mechanics cannot be translated into solo play, an automated A.I partner can be put in place, one that the player does not have direct control over but that still acts as an assistant. You will find that pretty much every cooperative game can be played solo but there are exceptions to this. Games with traitor mechanics, where one player is secretly working against the other players, often as part of the game's theme, don't lend themselves to solo play for obvious reasons. This can sometimes be circumvented by removing that element altogether or tweaking rules slightly, but more on that later.

There are also a number of titles that include a challenge mode which can be completed solo, for example a game could task you with achieving the highest score possible with X number of cards in your hand or may have a set number of challenges of increasing difficulty with success depending on your score. Sometimes the goal can simply be finishing the game in a set number of turns.

Sometimes games do not have a solo mode built in by the developer, in these instances, the internet is your friend as always, there you can find numerous resources that offer homebrew solo options.

It's testament to the rising popularity in solo gamers the amount of effort and skill that goes into some of these creations. Forums are filled with solo and collaborative efforts to create alternative modes that don't take away from the core experience of games that initially look impossible to play on your own.

These homebrew efforts can range from downloadable PDF's, printable cards and even the creation of apps that can run scripted scenarios or random encounters in reaction to the players actions. Quite often, these creations evolve through feedback from players to the point where they can be refined to be just as good, if not better, than developers' own efforts.

Very often, house rules happen accidentally. If a rule has been misunderstood at the time you were learning the game then you could go on playing forever without knowing you weren't following the official rules. Monopoly is a great example of this, no two families ever play it the same way.

Should you use house rules? Of course, if it makes the game fun then house rules are perfectly fine and sometimes necessary. Sometimes, if a session is starting to become stale, then you can chuck in a last minute house rule to keep things chugging along nicely or end it early.

# I'm still not certain what you mean by 'board' game! What gives?

Board games, or table top games, can come in many different forms, some don't have a board and some don't even require a table. They can come in multiple, huge boxes filled with plastic figures and enough counters to choke a dozen donkeys or in small, pocket sized boxes. Some even come in the form of PDF's for you to print and play at work while nobody's watching. Some games are heavily reliant on a theme to draw the player in while others can be abstract and within each genre there can be sub genres with subtle differences between each one.

## A word on themes

Oh boy we could write a whole other book on themes but the best way is to try and keep it as brief as possible.

## Don't be put off by a game's weird theme.

In the world of Cinema it can get a bit dull watching the same old superhero or horror movies *(or so I've been told)* sometimes you want to mix things up with a bit of German expressionism cinema , or a film about talking sausages…Board games are no different, in fact, they can make the mundane extra exciting!

Classic fantasy games can be great but there are tons more themes and genres to explore. Once you've crawled through all the dungeons and vanquished your thousandth goblin you could always take on a zombie horde, maybe go to space, conquer the world or find a corner of an obscure European region and build the best castle!

There are limitless board games and not a lot of common themes to go around so you will find that publishers tend to get creative when it comes to the settings of some of their games.

And it can be glorious. Who wants to fight a manticore when you can run a shipping container business? Why conquer the galaxy when you can manage the resources of your dairy farm while making sure your partner and child have enough bread to eat!

Some of the best games I've played have, quite frankly, the dullest themes. I find trains as dull as peas but heck if there aren't a couple of train based games staring at me from my shelf, tempting me with their solid, one more go, perfect gameplay loops.

You can make patchwork quilts, design stained glass windows and even tile a pretend wall and I reckon you will be as exhilarated as that one time you went paintballing and shot your best mate in the privates.

So if you see a brown box with a picture of a wonky cow or a serene stretch of arable land on it, don't automatically put it down, have a read, ask the nice people in the shop if they have played it. It's not all superman and leatherface you know.

You can also find a great variety within themes, it's okay if you love knights or horror because you will find a rich variety of mechanics within the games that, thematically, float your boat. It's ok to not like sheep farming, you do you!

While board game genres can be tough to get your head around, pigeonholing games into just one category is a bit like trying to nail a jelly to a tree. Let's take a look at some of the types of modern tabletop games available along with their solo offerings.

# GENRES

# Roll and Move

The place where most of us started, games where you roll a few dice and move a few spaces. These games tend to come with a board, which is a good start, and will usually have some form of looping path or one with a start and a finish.

Roll and move games can be quite passive when it comes to decision making, where the actions you take are often depending on where you land. As such they tend to be looked down upon by certain board game enthusiasts who point to the lack of decision making and dull themes that can put people off the hobby.

At this point I would recommend you don't let other people's opinions dictate what you like but it's true that I once looked at dull, roll and move games such as Monopoly and The Game of Life as the bottom of the barrel before I found that not all roll and move games are rubbish.

**Formula D** is a roll and move game with a fun racing theme that lends itself well to the genre. Strategy comes into play with the inclusion of mechanics such as changing gears or tires which can dictate the type of dice being rolled. It's still a fairly simple game and its familiarity can be a nice alternative to some heavier games further on in this book.

If you are looking to show friends that board games can be more than moving a pawn around a board picking up cash every time you pass Go then there are games that blend the familiar rolling and moving mechanics with other ideas. **Talisman** is a fantasy adventure where the player has freedom to move around the board's many tracks representing 'realms'. You can turn over cards and fight monsters by rolling dice and make a few basic decisions that can dictate which path the game takes next. The majority of the time may be simply moving around a board picking up the equivalent of chance cards and hoping you get something beneficial but it's certainly a step up from some of the more tried and tested 'classics' and its simplicity marks it as a good bridge between Cluedo and something far more interesting.

Unsurprisingly, solo offerings of roll and move are few and far between. Its competitive nature tends not to lend itself to the solitaire experience. However there are some creators doing some interesting things with the concept. **Nautilion** is part of a series of solo games in the Oniverse, a selection of solo and cooperative games with a distinct art style set in the 'Dreamscape'. Each stand alone entry sits within a different genre and I would recommend pretty much every one of them. Nautilion, though, manages to not only make a roll and move game viable for solo play but is genuinely a fantastic game.

You take the helm of a small Nautilion submarine and attempt to defeat the treacherous Darkhouse by sailing your submarine to his lair, the Abyss. You must do this before his crew of henchmen reaches your homeland, the Happy Isles. Not only do you have to be quicker than his crew, you also have to assemble your own crew on the way or suffer defeat.

It's basically a race where you and your 'bot' opponent start from opposite ends of a track and aim to get to the other end first.

On your turn you roll 3 dice and assign one of each of the results to your ship, the ship of henchmen and the Darkhouse himself. The number you assign to each ship dictates how far it moves along the track of numbered tokens that you randomly place in a trail leading from the happy isle to the abyss. Wherever you land you get to pick up that token and 'recruit' it onto your ship. The caveat is that, by the end of your journey you must have all nine numbered tokens with no duplicates or you lose the game. The twist comes in that wherever the evil henchmen's ship lands, that token is lost.

The third die, assigned to the Darkhouse, can cause him to inflict damage on your Nautilion, losing crew members. This means you are constantly forced to consider damage control when assigning die. Is it better to leap ahead on the track and get a headstart but risk not having enough crew by the end of your journey or use lower rolls that may allow you to fill your crew quickly, risking the evil henchmen descending on your home before you have a chance to reach your destination.

With only four copies of each number you have to try and plan which die you assign to each crew so as not to lose that precious number you need to the darkness before you get to recruit it.

The game comes with expansions that mix up the rules allowing for replay-ability and added complexity. Nautilion comes packaged in a lovely little box with incredible artwork, set up is easy and doesn't take up a lot of space. The perfect roll and move to have with a cuppa if you have a spare thirty minutes.

# Area Control

Controlling certain areas or the majority of the board, is the key to victory in area control games. One of the common examples of an area control game is the old classic, **Risk**. In Risk you bid for world domination by moving your troops into your opponents territory using simple combat rules where dice are rolled and the highest values win. More territory means that you can gain more bonuses in the form of more troops to use to battle your opponents, Risk is considered a classic war game in which you jostle with other players, staving off attacks on one side while looking to expand your power, choking the dwindling resistance from your opponents.

Area control isn't necessarily about dominating the majority of the map or board. Sometimes it's about the advantage a certain region may offer such as victory points or resources that can be used to build towards end goals. There is often a balance to be found in not spreading yourself too thin in these types of games to avoid being left drowning in the bitter soup of your own hubris. Like a fly that couldn't resist a sniff of your scotch broth despite there being a bread roll left unwatched on the kitchen counter.

**Carcassonne** is a little beaut of an area control game that goes about things a little differently. Firstly, the board is gone, replaced by a stack of tiles you place yourself, mapping out your own french landscape dotted with cities, roads, cathedrals and more. The area control part comes from using your limited number of meeples to 'claim' these areas, gaining points throughout the game depending on the size of the cities, lengths of the roads and other factors. It lacks the direct conflict of the more bloodthirsty Risk but is no less compelling *(and it's a lot shorter to play)*. There is also an official solo variant that can be printed from their website.

Both Risk and Carcassonne are considered entry level games that can offer hours of entertainment. Carcassonne with an absolute shed load of expansions that can tweak the formula in so many directions and the equally baffling number of licensed variants of Risk.

Area control mechanics, by definition, compel the player to seek out conflict and thrive on interaction. The tactical nature of out thinking your opponent may not necessarily lend itself to a solo situation. Fret not though as options are available for those who seek to take control of their own territory without having to elbow their opponent in the neck.

**Tiny Epic Defenders** is part of the **'Tiny Epic'** series. Another lovely set of small box games but this time with some hefty themes *(hence the Epic part)*. While most of the Tiny Epic series have a competitive edge Defenders is fully co-operative, therefore it is perfect for solo play.

Tiny Epic Defenders offers you the chance to play co-op by taking on the role of two characters or you can go fully solo by playing just one of the characters on offer. It's an area control game in the literal sense as you bid to defend your capital city and its surrounding six areas from an ever increasing onslaught of beasts that culminates in the arrival of the big bad epic foe. Take down the boss while defending your capital and you are a winner. If your capital is destroyed then bad luck.

Tiny Epic Defenders is won and lost on the decisions you make on which areas to move your meeple to so that you can either defend it from attack, a move that depletes your own health leaving you less effective for subsequent turns, or allow the area to fall to the enemy leaving you intact but your capital at risk.

At a fairly brisk 20 - 30 minutes play time, bad decisions tend not to stick around too much before you are starting another round, leaving you free to experiment with different approaches. It's also got enough variety when it comes to epic foes and character abilities to offer a good chunk of replay-ability.

Like most solo offerings, the challenge on offer can swing in the games favour at times, demanding a methodical and thoughtful approach but on the whole, it serves as a gentler and more enjoyable introduction to area control in general.

It's also fantastic with up to 4 players so can also be a great little intro to a group of friends who may see it as a gateway to some of the bigger box, competitive games.

# Deck Building/Card Drafting/LCG

The main mechanic of deck building games is creating a custom built deck of cards to defeat your opponents. These aren't your standard 52 deck of Jacks, clubs, spades and hearts though. Themes in Deck building games range from high fantasy to building forts in your back garden and fighting over pizza!

Each game usually starts with players holding a deck of basic cards, sometimes each player's hands are identical, other times it's the luck of the draw. In some games, the cards themselves can be currency to buy stronger cards or cards that synergise with those in your deck to either gain points or whittle your opponents health points down to zero to claim victory.

While in Deck building games you expand your deck for the purpose of repeatedly using your cards over repeated turns, card drafting is slightly different.

The main feeling of progression in deck building is the constant cycling through your deck, shuffling in newer, more powerful cards as it grows. The emphasis is on working out a balance as you steadily acquire new cards on the way to your goal.

In a deck builder, your turn may involve drawing a hand from your deck or playing and discarding those you may be unable to use that turn.

When your deck runs out, this is the opportunity you shuffle in the discard pile back into your deck along with all the juicy new cards you've purchased. Congrats, you have now created a bigger, stronger new deck to draw from.

Be careful though, buying willy nilly can clog up your deck with unusable, filler cards that will dilute your chances of pulling that awesome, game winning card you snapped up three rounds ago. Some deck builders have mechanics in which you can mill out your weaker starting cards from the game, the balance can come from identifying when it is best to keep a few of these cards sat in your deck for certain situations.

The absolute Grandad of deck building games is **Dominion**, the game that pretty much kick-started deck builders. In Dominion the aim is to finish the game with the most victory points. Each player starts with a deck made up of currency and estate cards.

Each turn players draw five cards from their identically small deck and may take two actions: Play an action card and buy a card from the available action cards or point scoring estate cards. Finally they place *(clean-up)* all cards used or unused into their discard pile so they are ready to be shuffled back into their deck when it runs out. The key is buying action cards that you can use in future turns that can grant extra actions on top of your usual one or even grant you extra currency or allow you to buy more than one card on your turn.

As you slowly build your deck to hold more action cards that help you towards your goal of securing victory points you will find that some card actions bounce off others, creating combos where you will be playing card after card, racking up points while grinning like the cleverest cat ever to learn to play tabletop games.

Dominion itself has spawned expansions that add to its already impressive 500 or so cards and is the influence to all other deck builders out there who have borrowed and expanded upon its key mechanics in interesting ways.

If you think deck builders seem built for competitive play then you are right, they can be great ways to fill an afternoon. And with a vast array of gateway options within the genre it shouldn't be too hard to convince someone to give one a go if you promise to go easy on them with your vast skills, you clever sausage you!

In card drafting games players usually start without any cards and get to choose from a common pool to play immediately or to hold on so that they can either 'build' something for points, such as in the game 7 Wonders, or fill railway routes with trains in Ticket to Ride. The trick to drafting games is not just looking at what you may need to further your goals but to observe your opponents and which cards they may be looking for. Fun can be found in denying them by taking cards you know that they need, if you're feeling spiteful of course.

A very family oriented and fun example of a card drafting game would be, **Sushi Go**. Each player starts with a handful of cards filled with gloriously cute little sushi creatures, each worth a variety of points depending on certain factors laid out at the beginning of the game. You can only pick one to take from your hand before you have to pass it to the player on your left. At the same time you receive a fresh new set from the player to your right. Thematically this is a wonderful recreation of the conveyor belt at a sushi restaurant that continues around the table until the players have drafted and built their own smorgasboard of sushi friends. After three rounds you total your scores up with one player being crowned the winner.

The strategy comes from the type of cards you choose. Certain cards only score if you have a certain number of that type, or, in some cases, if you hold the most. In some cases, cards don't score at all if someone else picked the same type of card that turn. There is fun to be had in denying an opponent that third sashimi card, rendering the two they have in front of them useless, even if you didn't actually need it... Diabolical!

Solo options are available too, **Mage Knight** takes both deck building and drafting to an absolute extreme and is widely regarded as one of the greatest solo games available. In Mage Knight the deck building element is mixed with fantasy, RPG mechanics, miniatures and more crunch than a Cadburys factory on a Friday.

You control one of 4 mystical Mage Knights *(the game can be played in co-op with up to 4 players but is still absolutely built for solo play too)* as you build your army and fill your deck with powerful spells and actions. You can explore dungeons and conquer cities in a really deep, if complex, adventure game. Mage Knight is a step up from smaller box solo games and as a result does have quite a steep learning curve. It's probably not the best idea to jump straight into a game with as many moving parts without sampling other, simpler games beforehand but it does hold a lot of rewards for those who persevere past its tough

exterior.

Back to smaller, solo offerings, **Star Realms** is an immensely popular competitive deck builder in which you purchase various spaceships each turn in a bid to build an armada capable of reducing your opponents influence points down to zero. Star Realms is simple in that each ship can either be used as currency to buy more ships or as combat points to attack your opponent. As you gain more ships you can combine the power of cards in interesting ways, generating currency to buy bases that can act as shields or unleash devastating attacks.

Star Realms Frontiers is a variant of the game that comes with a set of solo missions in which your human opponent is replaced by a variety of bosses that follow scripted attack patterns. These work almost like puzzles that you have to work through, building a deck that can break through some pretty brutal opponents while fending off their attacks.

There is a lot of fun to be had in working through the solo mode at its varying difficulties and It's a great way to learn the game with a cooperative mode also available. Once you've worked your way through this solo mode you will be left with a fantastic little deck builder with stacks of replayability and opportunities to expand with various new sets available to buy.

You may have noticed that we haven't got to LCG's yet and that's because they can have a bit of both the drafting and the building aspect. They also can be perfectly suited to solo play.

They can also be very expensive.

Living Card Games *(LCG's - a term coined and trademarked by Publisher, Fantasy Flight Games)* are collectible card games, a little like the Pokemon trading card game but where the packs are sold predefined with no rarity. This enables the buyer to know exactly what they are getting for their hard earned money. By doing it this way it creates a playing environment that can be crafted by the publisher to change as they release new expansions and modules to build upon the game, essentially creating a living game that evolves the more you play… and pay.

Examples of LCG's are, **Arkham Horror: The Card Game,** a title that see's players take on the roles of investigators fighting against the supernatural, Lovevcraftian horrors across various campaigns and modules. It's simple enough to pick up a starter set with enough cards for 2-4 players to take on a short, three act campaign, but the real 'living' portion comes in when you explore the masses of new, self contained campaigns that bring in new mechanics, monsters and investigators that layer on rules and twists like a big creamy tentacled trifle.

Of course, to get the most of these games you will always be chasing the newer stuff, which is where the expense comes in. Some campaigns can require you to spend at least a hundred pounds to see all of it, and that's if you can find all the packs that make up each 8 part cycle at retail as they can sometimes go out of print for a few months. Patience can pay off here or a quick look at the second hand market if you cannot wait.

There have been recent changes with the series that have reduced the amount of separate purchases required to enjoy a full campaign but be warned that LCG's can be an expensive hole to fall down if you are a completionist.

They can be worth it though and are perfect for solo play, as well as Arkham Horror, **Marvel Champions** is a great solo LCG with hero decks that enable you to take control of a variety of Marvel characters in a bid to foil the plans of famous villains from the universe.

It's a little more straightforward than the more complex mechanics of Arkham and, generally the aim is just to punch the villain a lot til his hit points reduce to zero but there are some advantages to choosing this over its, horror themed cousin. Firstly, it is far more generous in its pricing with the option to skip some hero packs you just don't fancy and with expansions that are all contained in one box without the requirement to buy multiple products. It's also newer which means that it's easier to find in retail so if you do want to try the starter set *(and like it)* you can pick up additional heroes and villains at a reasonable price.

# Engine Builder

This is where we start getting a bit clever, but don't let that put you off, engine builders are a bit like riding a bike, you might fall off at first, but once you are moving it's easy. These games rely on players taking actions to create a process that takes the resources and/or actions within the game and turn them into a steady stream of additional resources or points. These resources afford you more choice in later turns so you can build towards victory each round as your engine spits out more and more opportunities like a delightful little machine.

Make sense? If not an engine building card game usually goes a little like this:

- Collect a basic card on your turn
- Use that card to get two more basic cards the next turn that may allow you to get points.
- Use a combination of your basic cards to get a special 'rare' card

- Use that rare card to get even more points

Now every turn your opportunities to build a deck, or 'engine' to give you more points or better cards that do more 'stuff', increases. By the end of the game you are slamming cards on the table like a maniac, cackling over your lovely lovely points. Engine building games offer a "ramp up" effect where at the start you may feel feeble and weak but by the final round your turns are so magnificent you start forging yourself a crown.

Engine building elements are present in tons of games across every genre. In **Splendor**, you collect different coloured gems to purchase cards, or 'developments', from a shared pool in the middle of the table. These developments give you a permanent gem bonus which means you always have more gems to help you afford more expensive developments. These more expensive developments not only offer you higher gem bonuses but also prestige points and the ability to purchase 'nobles' cards that also offer a bigger chunk of prestige points. When one player gets to 15 prestige points, the game enters its final turn before the scores are counted up.

The engine building in Splendor is very light and basic. Collect gems to build developments so that you can then build better developments and efficiently gain more prestige points.

**Wingspan** is a card game in which you collect birds in your aviary represented on your beautifully illustrated player board. Your turn consists of one of 4 actions that, as the game goes on, result in cascading effects.

As the cost of collecting birds increases, the rewards do so too.

You can gain more food, or eggs (the little eggs are great, you'd be forgiven for wanting to pop 'em in your mouth but don't, they haven't got chocolate inside) and add more birds to your engine.

At the end of four rounds the scores are added together based on a variety of factors  including secret, random objectives that you were building towards that can help you focus on which of the limited avenues to prioritise and maximise the efficiency of your board.

Wingspan comes with an automated opponent mode, or Automa that mimics a real life player without literally having to play their turn for them. Instead you turn over a deck of cards that signify actions that they take, crucially this does not affect the way you play your part of the game, no systems or elements are removed when it comes to taking your turn so, for all intents and purposes, it is just like playing against a real person as they accumulate their own birds and related bonuses.

And Wingspan isn't the only engine builder that has a great solo mode. **Terraforming Mars** is a game where you compete against other corporations racing to be the first to make the red planet liveable by raising oxygen levels, creating oceans and raising its temperature. You do so by buying cards to gain resources that will, in return, help you get closer to your goals. The key to victory is building an engine that allows you to play more and more high value cards as the game goes on with each system in the game helping to ramp up your game winning parameters.

The solo mode has players playing against the clock rather than an automated player. This mode gives you a set number of turns to fully terraform your planet but adjusts some of the starting conditions to make it a little more difficult. It's definitely a change from the competitive aspect of the multiplayer mode and relies on players adopting different strategies while retaining its engine building core gameplay loop.

# Legacy

A legacy game takes place over numerous sessions with a single narrative weaving throughout what could be described as a campaign. The decisions made in each game can have permanent effects on subsequent sessions. Cards may be ripped up, boards may be written on and even new rules can be added to the rulebook as the game evolves. A lot of legacy games can only be played through once due to the permanent changes made to the components as sealed boxes and envelopes are opened, throwing up plot twists and developments unique to your own playthrough. Not all legacy games are over once you have played through its campaign. There are a number of titles in the genre that can still be played as 'forever' games long after you've finished ripping up cards or opening boxes. Titles such as **Clank** and **My City** leave you with your own unique environment to keep revisiting as much as you like.

One of the first legacy titles was **Risk:Legacy**, a twist on the classic war game where each faction can make temporary or permanent changes to the gameplay with some actions even destroying countries on the map. Playing through the 15 campaign missions with the same group of people is pretty much a necessity in Risk:Legacy as the decisions made by individuals impact the game in a major way. Unlike a lot of legacy games though, once you have finished your campaign you can restart, albeit with the board in the state you left it in. Or use it as a standalone risk board with the new rules in place.

Legacy elements are being added to a number of releases as the trend of creating a narrative continues. Smaller games are beginning to have campaigns added that allow longer, unique run throughs that can take place over a few sessions and more established titles have also followed suit.

**Pandemic** now has three seasons of their legacy series in which players work together to cure diseases spreading throughout the globe. In the original, standalone game you do this by moving around a map of the world removing disease cubes from cities and collecting cards of matching colours to eventually eradicate the threat. Of course none of this is straightforward as the game itself is working against you with its own deck of cards that will steadily fill the map with more disease cubes, triggering outbreaks and, if not managed efficiently, your inevitable defeat.

Continuing the tradition of Legacy games, there are boxes to open up at various points through your 12 sessions *(one for each month of the year)* each containing new additions to the story and elements that stack on one on another as cities are overrun by infection that can leave player characters 'scarred' or even at risk of dying and being removed from the game entirely.

As a co-operative Legacy game, **Pandemic:Legacy** is perfect for solo play as you are able to control 2 or more characters fighting an ensuing plague. It's true that some elements of the atmosphere may be lost by as you are unable to experience the unraveling story with friends. On the plus side, playing a solo legacy mitigates the hassle of getting together the same group to play each time you want to continue a campaign that could take months to complete.

One other awesome legacy game that can sing in solo mode is **Gloomhaven**, a game as heavy as a medium sized dog that comes in a box filled with enough cardboard to build a shed. This game is pure fantasy heaven as you take control of one of 6 starting classes that range from large brutes to small, mind controlling rat-men. Throughout its hundred plus hour campaign over 95 different missions you will have the opportunity to unlock 11 more small plastic miniatures, each with their own unique playstyle and deck of cards that you will use for both movement and combat. You will also manage your inventory for each character, purchasing upgraded gear and even, if you want, contributing some of your spoils to the town of Gloomhaven itself, unlocking more rewards and mysteries placed in sealed envelopes. The crunchiness of Gloomhaven's dungeon based combat actually makes it perfect for solo play as you are free to learn at your own pace and make errors without worrying too much about affecting other peoples experience.

Legacy and campaign games can be a time intensive commitment and the thought of ripping up cards and defacing something you've paid a lot of money for and that you won't likely be able to pay again may put some people off. Legacy games are more than just a game, they are an experience, and when you look at that way, what incredible value, £60 for 12 games is 12 evenings worth of entertainment, you find something else you'll want to do 12 times in a year that costs £5! I would urge anyone who is interested in modern, hobbyist board gaming to give one a try, it's definitely worth having one in your collection.

# Roll and Write

I've got to be honest here, roll and write games are probably my favourite type of solo game and they are the perfect medium to play alone.

As the name suggests, in roll and write games you roll something, usually a set of dice, and then you write the results down on a board or a pad. **Yahtzee** is the original roll and write game in which you roll 5 dice, use your results to score combos such as having three of the same number or a 'run' of consecutive numbers, jot your score on your pad and once all the sections are filled you add up your score and, if you are playing competitively, someone gloats while the other grumbles and thinks of places to stick 5 small cubes.

They are (usually) quick, require little to no setup and can range from devilishly simple to less devilishly simple but with a bit more added depth. They are also perfect for travel, to take on a short break plus, if you are struggling for storage space, they take up hardly any room so you can buy loads of em!

And if it's depth that you're after then oh boy can a roll and write offer up endless strategies, opportunities to push your luck while rewarding careful planning and enough moving parts nestled just beneath the surface of each of those thin sheets of paper to keep the game complex without making your eyes curl up!

In **Railroad Ink** each player is given a small, dry erase board with a grid that represents your city. On each of the 7 rounds you roll 4 dice each with different combinations of roads, railways and junctions. It's up to you to decide where you draw these networks on your board with the aim being to build transport lines from designated exit points on your grid that all interconnect creating a continuous network of roads and railways that snake across your board in perfect harmony.

But it's never as simple as that.

Often you will roll that one piece of road or rail that doesn't fit on to your perfectly organised route. So you start another network from the other side of the board, confident that you will be able to attach it to your existing infrastructure in a couple of turns.

But then you get something else that doesnt fit and you're left with half finished roads that go nowhere and railways that just stop... they just stop!

Points are scored for completed networks that have a clear entry and exit on one of the designated spots around the board. More points are on offer for your longest road or railway. Even more points are available if you use squares in the centre of the board causing players to risk venturing far from the safety of the edge in the hope they will get the right roll that enables them to make it to one of the exits.

Those dangly, half finished roads with no clear ending? lost to council budget cuts or heading off into the dodgier areas of your city? They lose you points, leaving you cursing that one roll that could have tied everything up neatly but instead left a scraggly mess filled with regret.

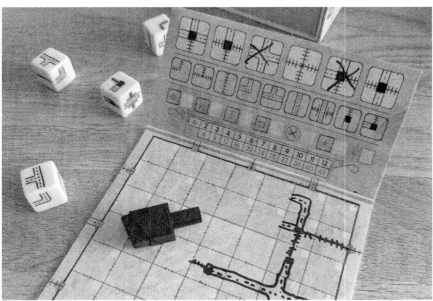

To get around this, at three points throughout the game you can use one of your extra intersections, lined up at the top of your board to tick off. With these you can save your pristine network from being the laughing stock of the next annual meeting of the transport committee and instead be awarded the grand prize for best railway and road person of the year! The satisfaction that comes from risking that extra network and managing to piece it all together with the clever use of a junction never gets old as you tell everyone that you planned it all along... You didn't.

This is an example of theme fitting the genre perfectly. It's like playing with a little train set that you can just wipe away and start again in lovely 20-30 minute sessions depending how quickly you can scribble. As a solo game there is no mechanical difference to playing it with others as there is little player interaction to begin with, it's just you, your little board and 4 chunky dice filled with possibilities.

Except, when there are 6 dice.

Each of the editions of Railroad Ink comes with a pair of 'expansion dice' These 2 extra coloured dice mix things up with rivers, lakes, meteors, deserts and more! Each expansion adds an extra scoring method and adds a little extra complexity to a brilliantly simple game.

And this is probably why roll and write games hit that sweet spot. Just like sitting down with a Sudoku or crossword puzzle, you can play one pretty much anywhere that you can roll a couple of dice and just like a book of crosswords or puzzles, the simplicity of its exterior can hide some fairly complex and even strategic elements.

For example, **Welcome To...** is actually a 'flip and write' game. Players turn over numbered cards and assign a number to each house in a 1950's US suburb. The hard part comes from ensuring that houses in each street go either up or down in numerical order.

Planning is a key aspect, in comparison to the random chaos of a Railroad Ink where your plans can be destroyed by the roll of a die,

Welcome To rewards a well thought out approach in which you plan your perfect neighbourhood with cards enabling you to build fences to create mini neighbourhoods as well as gaining extra points from pool and parks. You are still at the mercy of the card flips, but by playing the odds cleverly, you will be able to get yourself those sweet high scores.

In **Ganz Schon Clever (That's Pretty Clever)** you roll different coloured dice, placing the results on a pad that almost resembles a fruit machine. Each coloured dice belongs in its own section, each with its own 'rule' that, with careful planning, can build into chains of results that fill your colourful little machine up with even more numbers that can grant you extra dice rolls to maximise your all important end score.

All of these games play solo with little to no concessions made in comparison to the multiplayer game. So, if you like numbers, a bit of strategy or even just chilling out then a roll and write is the perfect addition to your collection.

# 4 X

4X games are named after the 4 crucial elements they are made up from, these are:

- **Explore** - revealing elements of the map or uncovering tiles through exploration.
- **Expand** - build upon these discoveries by claiming areas of the map to control.
- **Exploit** - Use these territories to gain resources, build and improve units or to increase your power.
- **Exterminate** - Engage with your opponent in some form of combat with the aim of taking theri resources, removing their units or eliminating them from the game.

This is a genre with a heavy link to classic strategy computer games such as **civilization** where strategy is king in planning your victory through a combination of those 4 X's that make up the game. As such there are loads of similarities between board games in this genre and their digital counterparts.

**Hyperspace** is a fast moving, asymmetrical game that ticks all 4 of the boxes. You start a game as one of a number of alien races (or Civ's) on a modular board made up of a number of face down pieces. Only each player's home world is uncovered holding their opening fleet of ships, a space station used to spawn more ships and a planet holding a number of resources. On each player's turn they can complete 3 actions from the choices available to them: Exploring to uncover tiles on the board, building (expanding) to place colonies on planets or producing (exploiting) to generate resources to build more ships or perks.

Now that you have explored, expanded and exploited new planets it's time to exterminate. Combat is pretty straightforward, you move your ships into a rivals and declare your intention to fight. Each player rolls a number of dice based on the amount and type of ships that are present and damage is dealt based on the results.

The key to victory in Hyperspace is balancing all of the 4X elements to gain victory points and once a player hits 15 victory points they can choose to end the game, at which point everyone calculates their final scores and counts up all the extra bonuses that they accrued through all their '4Xing'

The winner quite often is the person who used diplomacy and negotiation to worm their way to victory too. Hyperspace rewards table talk, alliances and back stabbing and as such is unfortunately not a game that can be enjoyed solo at the moment. It's likely that a solo mode will be developed in some form in the future but as it is a recently released title, one does not exist at this time.

### **One caveat here, a bit of a mea culpa I'm afraid**

*To explain this one fully I have to introduce the idea of Kickstarter for those who have never heard of it. Kickstarter is a crowd sourcing platform that has launched products of all different types. From gadgets to shot films, from books to smartwatches and, in this case, board games.*

*Kickstarter works on the idea that it isn't a store that you buy things from, it's a place where a creator will set a deadline for their project to hit a certain financial goal. Backers will pledge money based on various tiers that will go up in value. Using boardgames as an example, the smallest tier is usually a copy of the game for a set price with higher tiers included that will offer add-ons for more money.*

*If the project hits its financial goal then backers are charged the amount they pledged and the project is developed, manufactured and sent out to them.*

*There are a small number of cases, unfortunately, where projects may hit issues after the deadline and financial goal has been met. In many events this means delays but in others it can result in projects being cancelled or not delivering what was initially promised. In most of these cases you will get your money back but there are instances where your results may vary slightly.*

*Kickstarters for boardgames, especially big projects, are becoming more common now and, at the time of writing, Hyperspace is a project that has been beset by a number of delays with currently no fixed release date in sight. This is unfortunate as it is a good game and can still be played on some digital platforms such as TableTop Simulator (more on that later) but allow this to act as a word of warning when you look at shiny new games on crowdsourcing platforms that promise the moon on a stick.*

For a slightly heavier and time intensive take on the genre (and a game you can actually buy in a shop!), **Twilight Imperium**, now in its fourth edition, is another multiplayer only 4X game that can literally take a day to play. Factions seek to dominate the galaxy using their military might, diplomatic talents, and economic bargaining as they move their fleets, expand their empire and engage in battle with their opponents in an epic space opera that is different every time it's played. A little less heavy but also less time consuming is **Civilization: A New Dawn**, an adaptation of the legendary 4X video game series. Players will expand their territory, gain new technologies and even build wonders in a bid to rise above the other nations.

Each play-through is different due to modular tiles and individual agenda and victory conditions. It's a great, modern take on the classic 4X genre that doesn't out stay it's welcome and translates the 'one more turn' aspect of the video-game into a 'one more game' experience on the table

Actual, official solo rules are difficult to come by in 4X games but if you are willing to take another trip into space then there is gold to be found...... Space gold?

**Space Empires 4X** has it right there in the title, a 4X game in which you build an empire in space. It's a fairly traditional game with a big empty board filled with loads of hexes, small cardboard 'chits' to throw around with ships and planets on and a big sheet of paper to track all your various stats and technology trees, and yes, at first glance it looks as dry as a dinosaur bone made out of cream crackers.

If you look at Space Empires board and components and think you won't have a good time then you'd be wrong (unless you hate space of course) you'd also be wrong in thinking that the game will be a nightmare to learn. The game's fairly simple rules are laid out very clearly in its 8 page rule-book and handy reference cards. You won't need a space degree to get along with this one.

Player turns are made up of the usual 3, move some ships, explore the galaxy by turning over those chits, and combat. Once these turns are taken, an economic phase takes place in which players mine for resources on their existing colonies, spend resources on upgrades or new ships and even bid for who will go first on the next turn. With victory based on player elimination, Space Empires rewards aggression, so while there can be a lot going on in the game (and a game can last for a few hours) ultimately the game is heavily skewed toward the exterminate aspect of 4X games.

As you may imagine, this changes slightly in the one player mode included in the box. In the first of the two scenarios in the core game, you work to build your empire while fending off powerful doomsday machines. The enemies spawn at set points throughout the game, allowing you time to build an economy that is strong enough to destroy them before being overwhelmed. Just like the core game, this mode relies heavily on the exterminate aspect, perhaps veering slightly into wargame territory rather than traditional 4X.

The second one player scenario, Alien Empires, is far more in keeping with the core gameplay mode for multiple players. In this mode you take on 2-3 alien races, each with a homeworld that must be destroyed. Each race plays similarly to a human opponent with some of the mechanics stripped back. The scenario book dictates how the aliens react to your moves and their own behaviour in relation to their movement, research and ship building.

Both modes offer something refreshingly different and go beyond just dumbing down rules for solo players. Whether it's battling back a hoard of super powered ships or the attempting to out maneuver the Automa of scenario 2, there is plenty to keep one player happy.

Is Space Empires 4X for everyone? Maybe not, it can look quite sparse on the table and relies on a bit of imagination to immerse yourself in the theme. Despite its simplified rule-set and user friendly interface it also may be a step too far for players newer to the 4X genre. If however, you are well versed in tactical games and have experienced their video game equivalents, it's an absolute winner for solo play and one you may be able to convince a non gamer to get into with some hand holding.

# Eurogame

It's almost becoming an outdated term now but Eurogames (or Euros) are considered to have originated in Germany and usually focus on strategy over chance (Dice are a rare thing in a Euro). Euros usually include competitive elements but not necessarily traditional interaction such as combat. Usually the only interaction is the competition over resources on the board or victory points. While it's not always the case, themes in Euros can be considered a little dry and don't dictate gameplay much at all. Instead, the mechanics of the game are front and centre meaning that games with vastly different settings can play very similarly.

Rules can be very tight in a Euro and it's generally easy to learn the basics so that you can dive in and play quickly. They tend not to have any player elimination and players usually spend the game concentrating on their own area of the board meaning they can be fairly sedate and balanced experiences. Victory points are often added up post game and can depend on factors such as longest train track or largest field (I told you some of the themes can be dry). Euros are famed for post game scoring that can swing victory in your opponents favour or capture it from the jaws of defeat.

The Euro genre is stuffed full of classic games too, including a number of gateway games because of their streamlined rules. The aforementioned area control game, **Carcassonne**, named after the French fortified city (so far so Euro) tasks you with building roads, fields and cities amongst the French landscape. The gameplay is simple, you start with an empty table and stacks of small square cardboard tiles. You draw a tile and place a tile, slowly expanding your modular board with longer roads, larger cities and fields surrounding cloisters. Once you have placed your tile adjacent to a tile already on the table, you can place a meeple on one of the features of that tile. If you place your meeple on a road then they become a highwayman, in a city they become a knight, in a field they become a farmer and on a cloister, a monk.

Once the feature they are placed on is 'complete', that meeple scores the player some points. For cities, they need to be completely surrounded by city walls, roads must have a beginning and an end and cloisters must be surrounded on all sides, including diagonals, with tiles. Farmers don't score until the end game and gain points for every completed city that the field they are in connect to.

And that's the rules, you place a tile and can place a meeple, really simple. The strategy comes in the fact that you have limited meeples and only receive them back to be reused when their location has been completed. This means it is possible to run out of meeples and risk being unable to gain points until you draw the right tile. This is where the limited player interaction comes into play as you can purposefully scupper each other's plans by placing tiles that others may need in a totally useless place, forever damning their little wooden soldier to an eternity in an unfinished city…. so dark.

As a beginner game it works both as an entry into Eurogames and to modern boardgaming. In a couple of hours I managed to teach Carcassonne to my 3 children by playing one on one before we had a 4 player game where everyone was on an even playing field.

Carcassone has also received an official solo mode made available by German producer Hans im Glück. In this mode the emphasis switches from scoring the highest number of points to managing 3 different coloured teams that only score on a completed feature if they are the team with the least amount of points at that time. This restriction means that you are constantly considering the balance of each colour when placing your meeples on roads, cities or cloisters. Not only are you left juggling your team's points but making sure you don't run out of meeples, ending the game prematurely.

It's an interesting high score mode that breathes a bit of life into a game that can have a limited time on the table as you move on to more complex titles.

**Catan** *(originally known as **Settlers of Catan**)* is probably one of the most popular games in modern history and occupies the same space as Carcassonne as a great entry to the genre. Catan takes place on a board made up of randomly placed hexagonal tiles that each represent resources from wood to sheep! The aim is to accumulate 10 points by building settlements, gathering and trading resources and building roads. Catan does rely heavily on player interaction for trading so an official solo mode doesn't exist but there are many homebrew versions available on sites such as Boardgamegeek.

One of my first Euro's was **Ticket to Ride**. Like most Eurogames, you have a limited allocation of resources (in this instance, trains) and must place them on routes between cities. Before the game begins, each player pulls tickets with routes between 2 destinations that, when fulfilled, award you end game points based on its length. The penalty for not fulfilling them is the deduction of that same number of points, risk/reward!

Players draft coloured cards from a central, shared reserve and can only place their trains on routes if they have the required number of a specific colour to fill that route. The conflict comes from building up your hand to fill in that all important route only to have it snatched from you by a competitor.

Like most Euros, this is the only interaction between players and can lead to routes being fought over by a number of players, or at times, players going out of their way to block routes that others are looking to fill, just to halt their plans.

It's a game that can make veteran board game fans roll their eyes but in my experience I always enjoy it when it makes its way to the table even if it isn't always my first choice.

Unfortunately, the majority of solo modes for Ticket to Ride take away from the simplicity of rules that could be written on a train ticket and convolute them to a point in which the game becomes stale.

This can be an issue when relying on homebrew content for an euro game that relies so heavily on its competitive angle. So while I would always recommend it as a game for families to start off their collection, for the solo player, there are better options available.

The Euros I have already mentioned are all fairly simple, lighter games that can be great introductions to the genre. Make no mistake though, Eurogames can get pretty heavy and while **Scythe** certainly isn't the heaviest of them all, it's a step up in weight class from the others.

It also highlights the futility in even trying to categorise games in this genre as it has so many facets that could fit in a lot of genres but in its gameplay loop it heavily leans on euro characteristics.

In Scythe you control one of five factions in a fictional post war Eastern Europe. Your aim is to conquer territory across the map and build an engine that will reap the resources, build structures, enlist troops and eventually build giant mechs that will help you dominate the board and end the game with more coins than your opponent.

Player turns are quick in Scythe, on your turn you can complete one of the 4 action sections of your own player board. These sections contain two actions, a top and a bottom one, with the opportunity to complete both, if you have the required resources.

Each player's board is slightly different but will contain the same 4 top actions that range from basic movement, actions that make you stronger in combat and actions that give you resources.

Bottom actions are also similar but will offer different values in differing sections depending which board you are dealt at the beginning of the game. These are mostly used for upgrading the amount of resources you can gain, for building things to gain persistent bonuses or deploying those beefy mechs and building up that engine to

make everything more powerful.

These bottom actions include an upgrade option that can improve the resources gained from your 4 top actions, a build action that lets you place structures on the map which each offer their own benefits, an enlist action that unlocks persistent bonuses when taking other actions and a deploy action that unleashes up to 4 mechs on the board that allow you engage in combat and unlock powers such as crossing rivers, traveling longer distances or reducing any penalties that combat may impose.

If this already sounds like a heavy game then it kind of is, at least in comparison to lighter euros mentioned earlier. It doesn't take long to get used to though, ultimately your turn consists of doing only one thing and at the beginning of the game you will likely lack the resources to complete any of the bottom actions on your board. This means that the game flows quite quickly with complexity building as more choices become available. Once certain milestones are met such as deploying all 4 of your mechs or completing a set number of upgrades, you may place a star on the tracker on the board. As soon as a player accumulates 6 stars, the game is over and points are added up and converted into coins.

Now this is where the game adds more complexity. On The left side of the board is the popularity tracker, each faction starts with a different level of popularity which can be gained through certain actions in the game. Popularity dictates how many coins you get at the end of the game for each scoring category. For example, if your popularity is in the higher bracket then each territory you control at the end of the game is worth more coins than it would be if your popularity is in a lower bracket.

How can you lose popularity then? Well, one way to lose popularity is through combat. Only mechs or your player character can initiate combat, workers placed on the board cannot. Combat is initiated when you move one of your units onto a territory containing an opponent and is decided by a combination of your existing combat power and the secret playing of combat cards that can up your score. The player with the highest score wins, sending the opponents units all the way back to their base. The problem in attacking locations with workers on, even if there is also a mech there, is that this causes you to lose popularity (think of it a bit like a war crime in which a big bad metal beast attacks a poor farmer - naughty naughty).

So there is a lot to balance, a lot of fairly straightforward mechanics that all fit together to create a game where you seemingly always have options. You can race to build all of your mechs and get that star. Or, you can get your 2 combat wins out of the way early then shy away from conflict and aim to build your popularity to the max for another star and all the end game bonuses. You can even hoard those precious coins to get points on the board for the endgame while knowing you need to spend at least some of them to bolster your forces or produce valuable resources. With a few different combinations of faction powers and player boards available, there can be a lot of variety in a game of Scythe with no two games playing the same way.

Don't get me wrong, it's a fairly complex game and it took me a few sessions playing the digital edition against A.I opponents to grasp it. In fact I would perhaps recommend that method of learning if you have the option. If you do go for the physical box though (something i would definitely recommend as the components are particularly well made and it is a nice looking game) then you will have the option of a really well put together Automa opponent for solo play.

The Scythe Automa mode is an official mode in the box with its own manual and deck of cards that dictate the moves your opponent makes. There are 4 difficulty levels included ranging from an easy to ultra hard mode for those who believe themselves to be better than the developers.

Turns take place for the player in the usual manner, however your opponents moves are dictated by the top card of the Automa deck. Each card has a list of possible moves to choose from with preference always given to the first possible move that can be taken. Once this one move is complete any further bonus actions such as gaining coins are resolved. There are a number of additional rules that determine which of the moves the Automa takes based on various restrictions outlined in the manual. Other than a few further restrictions, they act in pretty much the same way as a human opponent, albeit their progress towards victory stars is on a set path dictated by drawing of certain cards.

It's a fairly jarring set of rules to initially get your head around but with handy reference cards and a clear logic to them, once you are used to them the game can move fairly swiftly.

Gameplay moves along pretty much the same as in a multiplayer game *(you can even play with multiple automa opponents)* with the only minor change to your own game coming in the post game scoring. It's this focus on retaining the core elements of the main game that make Scythe's solo mode a real benchmark, not just for Euros, but for tabletop games in general.

And if a really robust and replayable solo mode wasn't enough then Scythe's expansion, **Rise of Fenris** includes a full campaign that can be played fully solo across 8 scenarios that send the player searching for Nicola Tesla as strange new forces are seen around Europa. Each scenario offers new twists on the gameplay with narrative events affecting how you play and what impact is felt in subsequent missions. Without spoiling anything, there is a big chunk of game here that elevates Scythe's excellent solo mode into something altogether more special.

One thing about the solo mode, and especially Rise of Fenris, is the amount of book keeping that is required to manage an Automa opponent in a game that is already quite heavy with systems, cards and bits. There are unofficial apps available that can take a lot of this heavy lifting away by helping to manage a lot of the Automa, one particular app, Scythekick, is a big favourite among the playing community but other apps are popping up all the time. These homebrew methods can be a godsend when you are short of tablespace and can prevent you forgetting important actions.

The argument about what makes up a Euro can be summed up when it comes to Scythe. If anything it could be considered a 4X but the fact remains that it ticks a lot of the boxes of an old school Eurogame. Simple actions taken, albeit a lot of choice, minimal player interaction, no player elimination, a carefully balanced game and one that has multiple paths to victory.

Ultimately it doesn't matter which games you want to put in a divisive genre like the Eurogame, as board game designers seek to do new things there will inevitably be a blend of genres and the term will eventually become obsolete or maybe replaced with something a little more defined.

# Worker Placement

In this, slightly more complex genre, units, which are often thematically a worker, are faced with a range of tasks that they can be assigned to on each turn. This is usually done by placing them on a space on the board and claiming that task.

The tasks can start off as fairly simplistic such as generating a resource or completing a basic action. The tasks can then build, exponentially, developing into more complex actions that may create an engine, generating more resources, buildings that may give the player victory points or an infrastructure that carries the game to its resolution

Player interaction in worker placement games is fairly limited with the main competitive thrust being players jostling for a limited number of actions that they can benefit from. As such, it's a pretty great style of game to be played solo.

The worker placement genre houses some seminal modern board games, one of which is **Agricola**, a game that you'd be forgiven for dismissing if you saw it on a shelf due to its pretty uninspiring artwork and overall 'brownness'. It would also be pretty understandable if being turned off once you learn that, in Agricola, you are a farmer, in a shack, with a spouse, and eventually a family you need to feed. The majority of the game you will be taking such exciting actions as claiming wood, plowing fields and planting crops all in the pursuit of a bigger farm.

After reading that, you may even walk out of the shop, get in your car and drive home swearing at me when I also tell you that for the first couple of games you probably won't have much of a clue what you are doing and end up with minus victory points (or maybe that was just me).

The thing is, you'd be wrong to do all of that, and while I'm going to try to steer clear of this turning into a review of Agricola, you will soon see why it's considered one of the greatest worker placement games, if not up there as one of the best board games of all time.

Players start with two workers and these workers can only do one thing on each of the 14 rounds that make up 6, seasonal phases. Each phase concludes with a harvest round in which you have to feed your workers 2 units of food each or alternatively suffer the indignity of receiving a beggar card for every unit missed, each one of these cards taking points off your end game score.

To increase your work force you have to expand the rooms in your shack so that you can add children to your family. The bonus of an extra action per turn is balanced with the cost of having an extra mouth to feed when harvest rolls around. And here is an extra kicker. That harvest round comes around quicker each phase meaning you have less time to ensure you can feed your family each season.

So each round you decide where to place your worker so that they can claim the materials on that board space. Do you go for wood to quickly add rooms and eventually fences to house the animals that your next worker is going to claim? Do you plow fields to grow crops knowing that every unused patch of land on your player board at the end of the game will deduct more points from your total? Oh god you really need to bake some bread with all that grain or you won't have enough food to feed poor Archibald when harvest time rolls around.

And all the while, in the multiplayer game at least, your fellow players are vying for the same resources as you, forcing you to act early on the growing pile of materials that increases more and more each turn. If you just wait one more round then there will be enough to upgrade your house meaning more victory points but you just know that Uncle Eric is going to swoop in and get them before you, the absolute swine!

Throw in occupation cards that are different each game, offering buffs and upgrades as well as improvement cards that build ovens and workshops and you have a really tightly focussed game that weaves the initially overwhelming number of options you have into a series of opportunities to play around in a fun little sandbox.

It's practically impossible to have a perfect game of Agricola, other players won't allow it, but that's okay because you will have a chance to ruin their plans too. And in having to make the best of a bad situation, you learn other paths, other combinations that may work even better than what you thought you needed to do.

The solo mode is an ideal tool to learn more about it too, it's a simple score attack campaign in which the target score increases after each game. If you manage to beat the score by a certain amount you get extra food for the next round as well as starting buffs that keep the replayability alive. It may seem uninspired at first, and you do miss the competitive aspect of racing to get your workers placed on certain spots first, but it allows you to see how all the mechanics fit together at your own pace. Maybe on this playthrough you will concentrate on occupation cards to build an engine that will take away the anxiety of scrabbling for food in the final stages as your family threatens to outgrow your capacity to harvest crops. You could spend opening turns plowing fields and stockpiling grain as the wood, clay and reed resources increase in volume waiting for you to swoop in and collect them all in one go…. Take that Uncle Eric!

If you are after a worker placement game, Agricola should arguably be your first port of call. Even if there are games that have refined the formula since or perhaps offer a little more when it comes to solo play, you really should give it a go. And, if I'm honest, I think it looks pretty nice and the farming theme fits the gameplay perfectly.

That being said, **Viticulture** is possibly a more well rounded solo experience.

It's a game about growing wine, played over a number of rounds that represent years. Each round is split up into seasons *(board games love a season)* where you will place your workers to complete various tasks on your vineyard. There are some interesting mechanics in the game including how players decide turn order for each round, players who choose to act later can receive bonus rewards meaning that trying to get in there and place your workers early may not always be the best way.

So in Spring, turn order is decided, before players move on to summer where they will work towards victory points, primarily by placing workers to grow grapes in the fields, harvest them by placing clear grape tokens in the relevant red or white crush portion of their player board and eventually into their cellar where they can be used to fulfill order cards that can be drawn by, you guessed it, placing worker tokens on relevant places on the board.

The way that seasons beyond spring work is that the board is split almost vertically into summer and winter actions. At the beginning of the year, each player has a limited number of workers that they can place, once a worker is assigned a task in summer, they cannot be used again to perform a winter action. Now these actions include, training more workers, conducting tours for money or building structures and paying the monetary cost so that you can grow better grapes. You can increase the size of your wine cellar to include more expensive wines or build a cottage so that more visitors can be invited in the autumn phase to gain some extra special benefits.

The theme in viticulture is extremely well implemented. It oozes atmosphere and looks as tasty as the wines you will be brewing (Fermenting?) up in your big delicious wine baskets each year. There are some really clever mechanics such as Grande workers. These are extra large meeples that, once per year, can shove their big chunky frames on portions of the board already filled with other players, Viticulture is a game interested in balance where players can be free to explore different routes to victory without worrying too hard about missing out on actions that will prevent them having a chance at winning.

At the beginning of each season, an Automa card is flipped over indicating where they will place their workers. These workers are placed purely to block your progress as you have seven rounds to surpass the Automas' score. The solo mode also throws in another great mechanic where the seven rows of turn order (each with their own rewards based on the order you choose to take your turn) need to be used at least once during the game. This adds a further tactical element in which you can choose when to trigger the various bonuses for maximum effect. Such a simple addition opens up what can, at times, be a fairly tight experience where it can feel that there is an 'optimal' route to victory.

The excellent solo mode that involves the use of an Automa means that, for the most part, gameplay is pretty much unchanged from multiplayer mode. It's a really novel way of doing it though with the Automa sitting at 20 points from the beginning of the game, which is, interestingly enough, the number of points needed in the multiplayer mode to trigger the end of the game.

This solo mode would be pretty good in itself but Viticulture includes a solo campaign that doesn't just increase the number of points needed but introduces scenarios and criteria that must be fulfilled to win. These can range from the removal of certain types of cards to rules that dictate how many workers you must have at the end of the game.

The core systems in Viticulture work so well that the ability to adapt to a random Automa trying to ruin your year is immense fun to figure out because it always seems it's possible to do so. As a tool to figure out the game, the solo mode is great, but as a way to pass the time, having actual fun? It's perfect.

An honourable mention has to go to **A Feast for Odin**, now I'm not going to labour too much on the rules of the game too much apart from to put it out there straight away.

## A Feast for Odin is a heavy game!

It's certainly not the heaviest, crunchiest game out there and there are likely to be some veteran board game players who think it's pretty light and breezy. In it's defence (and it doesn't really need a defence, by all accounts its a great game that is highly acclaimed) it's arguably the game that's done the best job of balancing all that crunch with the fun aspect and, quite bizarrely also managed to be accessible enough to learn after a few playthroughs.

It's the usual worker placement, this time with a viking theme, but everything is cranked up beyond eleven! Your player board looks like an excel spreadsheet has crashed, the worker placement board resembles a medieval end of year tax report and there are so many bits you can buy, harvest, plunder or build that it takes two trays to hold them all. Quite frankly it's arguably the best in the genre right now but for new players it's probably all a bit too much.

The solo mode may not have a campaign but it does have you control two different coloured batches of meeples, taking turns, blocking the other factions choices each turn as you try to balance the games systems to gain an overall high score.

This brings out the more puzzle aspect of Feast for Odin and focuses you to look at the massively bigger picture as you maneuver your stock, tetris style, on your player board, planning ahead as you work towards items that will help cut off those pesky squares that take away from your final score. All the while racing to feed your viking tribe. The mode never feels random or unfair (although there is a little bit of dice rolling) and there is more than enough variation to ensure longevity on the table.

Solo

# Push Your Luck

Everyone has played a variation of blackjack at some point, right? It's you against the dealer with each of you trying to get the numerical sum of your cards closest to 21 without going over. Maybe you hold at a 10 and a 7 hoping that the dealer can't make a number between 18 and 21 with his cards. Or maybe you try one more, hoping for a 4 but, almost inevitably, get a 5... That's push your luck games.

The simple nature of a push your luck game is the main draw for me, seeing how developers can play with this most basic formula, adding twists and rules that make you sit up and pay attention helps to keep the genre fresh and exciting.

One of the earliest push your luck games I played was **Pass the Pigs**. I loved this game, it's a little travel case with inlays for the pig shaped 'dice' a couple of pencils and a pad to keep score, true nostalgia!

In the game, you rolled the little pigs, taking note of the scoring position that they landed in. If they ended up in one of the scoring positions on the handy rules sheet such as the 'double snouter' or the 'leaning jowler'. You could choose to bank the points or you could roll again and try to score higher, risking a result that could see you lose the points on that turn, your total points for the game or even eliminating you altogether.

Instead of rolling dice or pigs for luck, **Quacks of Quedlinburg** tasks the player with pulling tokens from bags. In Quacks, players are dodgy medieval chemists making potions from mystery ingredients trying not to overload their brew with explosive cherry bombs that can ruin their chance at victory at the annual... make a nice potion festival!?

At the beginning of the game, everyone fills up their lovely ingredient bags with a few cherry bombs and pumpkins. They then simultaneously, without looking, pull each chip, placing those with a higher face value further round the swirling score tracker of the cauldron. Each chip is numbered and cherry bombs are numbered either a 1. 2 or 3. If, by pushing your luck, the sum of all the cherry bombs in your pot exceeds 7, it explodes and you are only allowed to choose to take points or coins from your ruined brew. Players who manage to avoid disaster get to take both, using coins to purchase new ingredients that offer new perks and methods of pushing your potion to new limits as well as racking up the victory points to win the game.

Over nine rounds your bag fills with possibilities, mushrooms can be place further along your score track depending on how many pumpkins you have in your potion at the time, crow skulls allow you take a further two chips from your bag and choose which one you want to use and which one you want to put back with no penalty, black head moths give you a headstart on your potions or even valuable gems should you be the player who has the most of them in your potion at the end of the round.

The ingredients list is customisable too, with each having a second variant that allows you to mix and match effects, keeping the game fresh each time.

And you will likely play a lot, the fact that you know what's in your bag and have worked out the odds of success only to be absolutely shafted by pulling 4 bombs out in a row, doesn't seem unfair because you only ever have yourself to blame for pushing things too far.

Quacks expands brilliantly throughout its gametime. In its first few rounds players add ingredients to their bag and, with the confidence of somebody who knows exactly what they are dealing with. They manage to balance the luck pushing, knowing when it's safe to pull and when to pump the brakes. But as more ingredients enter your bag, you begin to forget what you've put in it.

Suddenly you are less confident, blindly rummaging around trying to work out exactly how many mandrakes you put in there or if it's worth risking tipping over that threshold for a couple of single point pumpkins.

Quacks is filled with moments of hilarious frustration and as such it does sing with a group of 4 people. However, there isn't a lot of player interaction in the game outside of mocking your opponents' failed concoctions, and while it is a competitive game with a score track, there is an option available for solo players.

It's not an official mode but there is an app available that does pretty much what a real life opponent would do. It's a simple thing, not an A.I as such but a tracker that gives you the result of your opponent's potion each round.

It's something that works well and takes little away from the core mechanics used when playing with real life opposition. Push your luck games rely on your decisions so having an automated opponent is just as good, and a lot less embarrassing when you inevitably cock up again.

**Pandemic: The Cure** has an objective that differs to most games in the genre in that it isn't a score based victory condition. This dice based spin off works similarly to the core Pandemic game in which players work together in a race against time to cure 4 diseases.

This version tasks players with rolling character specific dice that dictate the actions they can take. When treated, the diseases that are represented by coloured dice, are moved from the board into a quarantine zone. Once they are in this zone players need to roll their dice again to hopefully move these disease dice back into a bag of dice, lovingly named the 'infection bag'. The reason you need to be placing dice in this bag is because you will be regularly pulling more and more disease dice from here and once it's empty it's game over.

So you are regularly making sure the infection bag is kept topped up with nasty infectious dice, but how bout eradicating these diseases? The cure mechanic can only be done if a player rolls a vial icon. This dice is then spent and a die in the quarantine zone can be placed on the player's board. Once you have a multiples of the same coloured die you can choose to roll them in an attempt to cumulatively roll above 13. Do so and that disease is cured.

Play continues with more infection dice being placed on one of the 6 locations around the board. These infections can lead to outbreaks that spill into neighbouring locations, eventually overwhelming the players if left unchecked. So where is this, push your luck mechanic? You have the ability to re-roll your dice as many times as you want but the issue is that each dice has an infection marker on it. If an infection marker is rolled, that die cannot be re-rolled and the infection tracker in the centre is moved one space. When the tracker gets to the end, it's game over. If you haven't rolled the result you desired from your 6 dice, a re-roll puts the game in jeopardy as the likelihood of rolling game ending infection markers increases.

As a co-op game, Pandemic: The Cure translates perfectly into solo mode, playing multiple roles works well and, unlike the core game, doesn't give too much advantage in terms of coordination as you are generally at the mercy of a roll or your own nerve in pushing your luck to achieve the result you need.

# Wargames

Surely games about war need multiple players, I hear you say, and you would mostly be correct but there are a number of options available for solo play.

Wargames are pretty self explanatory and, as a genre, it's pretty hard to pin it down to specific mechanics as it is generally more of a theme than a genre. Wargames can take place on massive tables filled with miniatures where the victor is decided by a mixture of cunning and dice rolls and they can also be smaller, tense political head to heads such as **Twilight Struggle** in which players take on the role of either the United States or the U.S.S.R during the period directly after World War 2. In this fairly complex game, cards are primarily used in two ways, firstly they can be used to gain influence in countries across the six areas that span the globe. Secondly they can be used for their 'event'. These events mirror real life incidents throughout the time of the cold war and directly offer an advantage to either America or the Russians. The interesting element comes from players holding cards in their hands that can benefit their opponent if played at the wrong time and making the decision when to gain those all important influence points without giving your opponent a boost in their fight for domination.

The game is played on a sprawling board and has strong area control elements. Influence tokens are placed on countries in an attempt to wrestle control from your opponent. This isn't done through direct conflict but by thinking a few moves ahead, playing the right event and using different tactics throughout its 2 - 3 hour play time. While some form of heavy handedness can be used, this advances the defcon tracker and if this tracker hits defcon 5, nuclear war erupts and the guilty party loses the game.

Twilight struggle really is a thinking person's war game and is a history lesson in itself. Its slow burn may not be to everyone's taste though and, as a physical product, it's not particularly well suited to solo mode even though there is a pretty well made solo variant available that can be downloaded separately. I have found most of my enjoyment has been derived from the excellent digital edition that offers a pretty brutal A.I, perfect for learning the game in the event you manage to convince a real person to play it with you.

If something a little more shooty is up your street the **Undaunted** series leans more towards direct conflict. The games use deck building mechanics and modular boards placing you and your opponent in direct conflict though a campaign during World War 2. On the board, your tokens represent your platoons out on the battlefield. In your hand, the cards you draw each turn give you the chance to take actions with their corresponding token.

Objectives vary throughout each game's campaign with each subsequent scenario adding an extra layer of complexity and choice as new units are added, each with new actions. In the case of North Africa, vehicles were added to the conflict, giving players more tactical options.

In Undaunted, the choices you make can consist of when and where to move and which units to attack (an action resolved by a satisfying dice roll mechanic that can, and does, often go spectacularly wrong). Other actions bring in the deck building aspect in which you can recruit new cards to add to your deck and eventually into your hand which means you can add new units to the board.

Undaunted is a slick and well structured series of games that builds on itself throughout the campaign and offers replayability through its tight gameplay and deep tactical options.

For an official solo mode you will need the expansion, Reinforcements. This box also gives you the option to add an extra 2 players to the game and have teams. If you don't fancy shelling out for an expansion, homebrew solo mode's have been developed, one of which has a streamlined A.I table outlining the moves taken by your opponent based on the circumstances.

A different type of Wargame altogether takes players to the woodlands in **Root**.

Root is an asymmetrical fantasy wargame with area control and engine building elements. Players control one of 4 animal factions who all battle, in their own way, for control of the forest.

Each of the four factions in the base game (there are 10 in total with additional expansions) has the same victory condition, achieving 30 points, but they all do this in vastly different ways.

Strap yourselves in, you're about to go cross eyed again!

*Note* We are talking about base game factions here. To offer full breakdowns of each faction in the expansions and how they fit together would require its own book!

The Marquis de Cat are the present rulers of the forest having taken control from the birds of the Eyrie Dynasty. They start the game with presence in every clearing of the forest, an impressive army and sawmills providing materials each round for them to build recruitment centers for more troops, more sawmills or workshops to give them extra valuable points. A player controlling the cats has the task of bullying everyone else and building up their empire.

The Eyrie Dynasty play much differently, they start in one corner of the forest and must build roosts that give them points at the end of each round with the additional benefit of enabling them to enlist more birds to slowly spread throughout the board.

The main difference however is how they take their turn, these birds have a 'government' with a leader and a decree on how they will act each round. This declaration is set by placing 1 or 2 cards each round either in the recruit, move, battle or build sections of their player board.

Once these cards are committed to an action they must be strictly followed each turn. For example, each clearing on the board is a space in which players can build, battle, recruit or move from and to. Each clearing has a symbol, a fox, mouse or rabbit, that relates to the suits of the cards each player holds (there is a 4th suit, birds, which are wild). So if you place a card with the fox suit icon into the battle portion of your decree, each turn you must battle in a clearing with the fox symbol in it. If you decide to use a bird card in that portion of the decree then you are free to fight anywhere but, you must fight. If you can't or if you fail any other step of your decree then your government goes into 'turmoil' meaning you lose valuable points and any cards in your decree, having to start putting it together again.

So the Eyrie are more restricted than the Marquis de Cat in that they can only do what their decree says each turn but, with some good planning they can put together a string of moves that can be devastating to other players as they move, battle, build and recruit multiple times on their turn. The key to winning with them is thinking ahead, the key to beating them is trying to disrupt their plan.

So we already have a really interesting dynamic with two very different styles of gameplay slotting in together. The woodland alliance is there to fight both of these power houses through guerilla warfare!

The plucky rebels start with no troops in the forest but draft cards that they use as supporters. Firstly they use these cards to place sympathy tokens in the relevant clearing (based on the suit icon of the card). These sympathetic regions now force any player entering them to pay that player a card that they can then use to build more support for the woodland alliance.

As these sympathy tokens spread throughout the forest, the player can use their expanded arsenal of support cards to trigger rebellions in specific clearings. This action immediately removes any opposition from that clearing and a base is built there. Once a base is built, generals can be trained and the influence of the rebellion can spread even further. If allowed to build all 3 of their bases, the woodland alliance can quickly spread throughout the forest, strangling enough points to roll toward victory, Viva la revolution!

The vagabond is the 4th faction in the base game who takes advantage of the chaos emerging in the woodlands and moves silently from clearing to clearing using the woods themselves as cover.

With the ability to pretty much go anywhere, the Vagabond is a solitary unit that doesn't build bases or spread influence. Instead he crafts and collects items, gives support to factions of his choice in return for more items and indulges in a bit of espionage by destroying rival units or buildings making him public enemy number one.

The vagabond can even complete quests, building up his horde of items to fulfill goals in return for more cards or victory points. A player playing as this faction isn't interested in such petty things as conquering the woods, he thrives on chaos and the only way to stop him is to… well it's to stop him ruining your plans. That's not an easy task when he can ally himself with a rival faction and share victory, picking at you in return for protection.

I'm not going to go into details on combat, crafting and alternate victory conditions because even that, fairly, brief overview of each faction is probably more information than you can take in without either watching a playthrough, reading the actual, really well put together rulebook or simply just playing it. Which is something you probably should do if any of that sounded remotely interesting. Don't let Roots' awesomely cute artwork and adorable meeples trick you, it's a cut throat war game in every aspect.

It's also a bit of a pain to teach a group to play if they have no clue what's going on. As soon as you have learned enough about each faction to teach friends and family, you are instantly at a huge advantage when playing against them. Unless you are joining a group of people all coming at the game with an equal amount of knowledge, it's going to be a bit tough to have actual fun.

Which is why the solo 'clockwork' mode added in the form of an expansion *(which is unfortunately sold separately)* makes it worth adding root to your collection as a solo gamer. The box comes with automated versions of the four base factions for you to take on. These come in the form of new player boards that clearly display the actions they will take each turn based on cards drawn each round. This is a clever, robust and surprisingly complex A.I that takes a while to get used to but seriously offers an experience as close to playing multiplayer as possible. One huge advantage to the clockwork expansion is that it allows you the opportunity to play as factions you may have missed out on otherwise.

In the base game, you need to have players play as either the Marquis de Cat or the Eyrie. If you can only manage to get one player to your table this means you miss out on some of the other factions, including the other really interesting expansion factions that I won't go into details here *(okay.. There's lizards, otters, ravens and moles that all bring some crazy gameplay to the table)*. With the clockwork expansion taking care of the more 'basic' factions, you can be free to experiment with the exciting shiny new animals meaning that Root as a solo game has so much replay value it's unreal But it's also can get a bit expensive.

So yeah, the elephant in the room *(elephants?... they can't be in the woods!)* is the fact that you do need to purchase an expansion to enjoy root solo and that may put people off. The alternative is the excellently well put together digital version that enables you to play against bots or players online. It may be worth choosing that as your first option to test whether you enjoy Root as it's definitely not for everyone.

# Dungeon Crawler

A dungeon crawling game is usually a cooperative experience where players band together to explore an environment on a quest to maybe loot some treasure, kill a monster or maybe just escape. As the name suggests, this is usually in some form of fantasy dungeon but they can take place in all sorts of environments from space freighters to haunted mansions.

In **Descent: Journeys In The Dark**, one player takes on the role of an overlord attempting to thwart the hero's journey deep into their dungeon over a series of quests that can be added to with various expansions. Like most dungeon crawlers, Descent has lovely, crafted miniatures that players maneuver through the dungeon on their turn, fighting monsters with the aid of custom dice on their race towards the target. The overlord controls the monsters, throwing obstacles in the hero's way by performing a number of actions on their own turn.

Dungeon crawlers are all about atmosphere and Descent nails that aspect. It can be a little basic in terms of mechanics but that makes it a great starting point and there's enough content in the base game to keep players entertained before they even think about the many, many expansions.

As a solo experience, Descent has an official app that takes on the role of the overlord. This leaves you free to control one or more of your heroes with the app providing scripted events and instructions on how to progress through the quest. This includes unveiling the map as you pass through each room. The game board is modular, meaning that you add pieces as you move. This gives a great sense of mystery to your time with the game as the app can spring surprise monsters or traps on the player as you open doors or chests.

Recent re-release, **Descent: Legends Of The Dark,** jettisons the player controlled overlord and moves it all on to the app. This makes the newest version entirely cooperative and as a result, very solo friendly.

Descent can be a great introduction to dungeon crawlers then with the aid of the app, for the original version of the game, more content is available online for some of the expansions that the app doesn't cover. It's a real option for solo players who want to get some dungeon crawling done.

In **Nemesis** the fantasy dungeon is transported into space as players wander a hulking vessel inhabited by some pretty nasty aliens that they must escape from. If you have watched any of the popular horror sci fi movie series that began in the 70's then you pretty much know what to expect here.

Again we have miniatures, lots of rooms and corridors as well as items to equip and roles for the player to take. As a more modern dungeon crawler, nemesis adds a few more mechanics to the mix so it's not just hitting beasts and picking up treasure.

There are a couple of ways to 'win' in nemesis. One is to make it to the escape pods that need to be unlocked by activating the ship's self-destruct sequence or, in a wonderfully thematic twist, by having a crew member die! Another way to win is to simply return to the cryosleep you were rudely woken from. This however requires players to firstly ensure the engines are working, secondly make sure the ship is still heading to earth and not the middle of the sun and finally the players need to survive half the game's number of rounds without being eaten.

Each character has a set of cards that define what actions they can take, each offering their own strengths and weaknesses and they need to work together to make sure all of the steps needed to escape are completed before time runs out, or they are all scoffed by the alien.

The problem is, maybe they aren't all working together at all.

Nemesis has a traitor mechanic that can activate the first time you encounter the aliens. At the beginning of the game you are given two objectives, one is fairly general and the other is a bit more treacherous and can include singling out certain players to die or even for people to be infected *(Nemesis has a mechanic where you can gain infection cards with text that can only be read by the in game scanner ... well, a card with some red acetate on.. Still.. Pretty cool)*. Players decide at the point all hell breaks loose which objective to pursue which can cause tension as paranoia kicks in.

Solo mode understandably removes the traitor mechanic and includes its own dedicated solo objective deck. The game scales really well to one person and being a co-op game you have the choice to control multiple characters without the atmosphere being lost in the absence of other people around the table.

As a dungeon crawler, Nemesis does pretty much what every game in the genre does but really leans into its theme by adding new and interesting twists pulled from its clear inspiration from the Alien franchise. Its campaign will keep a solo player busy for a long time if they are fans of the source material.

# Storytelling/RPG's

Another slightly 'floaty' genre, storytelling games rely on a narrative to hook the player in and can pretty much have any mechanic included. Fancy a political negotiation game in which each player represents a 'house' in a Game of Thrones style fantasy universe? A game in which you draw cards describing a dilemma that you must argue and spend your political power on to resolve in a way that favours your own manifesto? The Kings Dilemma is likely way up your street, depending on whether you manage to pull together the recommended 4-5 players required to play through this gripping legacy game filled with a deep and rich storyline spanning generations of rulers.

If you want to sit down with a calming beverage or 3 and have your brain worked harder than a 24 hour burpee challenge then, **Sherlock Holmes: Consulting Detective** may be the answer.

Each entry in the series gives you 10 original cases to solve, all set in Victorian London. There are no dice to roll, no board to place a meeple with a deerstalker on, you simply get a map of London, a directory of businesses and a booklet for each case each with its own

front page of a newspaper for that day.

The game works a little like a choose your own adventure game but with much more sleuthing. You read the intro for the case and then are free to explore as you see fit. Visiting different locations on the map or 'contacts' in the Holmes universe leads you to different sections of the case book where you may be given a vital piece of information or hit a dead end in your investigation, forcing you to rethink your angle towards cracking the case.

Once you have exhausted your leads or decided you know who the culprit us, you turn to the back of the case book and are asked a number of questions ranging from who actually did the crime to various other points around how, why and even questions around some dangling loose ends that may have been uncovered throughout your investigation.

Once the questions are answered and the case solved you get the opportunity to hear from the man himself. Turning to the back page, Sherlock waltzes into the room and lays the case out in front of you, making it all seem so obvious and clear how he managed to deduce exactly what went on. You then compare how many locations you visited during your investigation and compare it to Holmes' number. For every extra step you took in your game you take 5 points off your final score and for every step you took less than Sherlock (not gonna happen, he pretty much nails it every time) you get to add 5 points. If at the end of the case you have more than one hundred points then you've beat Sherlock. If, like me, you end up on minus figures then?.... You have still had a great time.

As a solo game or a game for couples, the Consulting Detective series really shines. The puzzle aspect, working in a pair like the titular Homes and Watson suits this particular corner of the genre really well and if you have a partner who may turn away from tabletop games with counters or meeples then you may have better luck reeling them in with a couple of good old fashioned books. Should you opt for solo play however then you are missing nothing, in fact, this series is often lauded as the quintessential solo experience, just you, a bran baffling case and an evening or afternoon to solve it, Perfect.

Stories in tabletop games are nothing new. In fact, the Consulting

Detective series has been around since 1981, but one other story driven tabletop experience has that beat.

We are, of course, talking about **Dungeons and Dragons**.

Introduced in 1974 and now in its 5th edition, D&D is often used as the shorthand description for tabletop RPG's and is firmly steeped in popular culture. All you need is a set of polyhedral dice, someone to be DM (Dungeon Master) who serves as storyteller and enforcer of the rules, as well as a sourcebook or two to provide additional stats and scenarios.

The added ingredients are an imagination and a group of like minded individuals willing to go on a journey that can either take a couple of hours or unravel over a campaign lasting months or even years.

There is a lot more to tabletop RPG's than the fantasy worlds of D&D though, with properties such as popular video games, TV shows, movies or book series' spawning their own tabletop versions.

There is also a vibrant indie scene tackling a broad range of genres and issues from immigration to vampires (and one that tackles both). There are titles that reduce the amount of dice or remove them completely. It's within this indie scene that you will find a wealth of solo RPG's.

The creative aspect of playing an RPG really comes to the fore when playing solo. In games like **Gentleman Bandit** you end rounds by writing thirteen line poems as the titular gunslinger based on the events dictated by drawing from a standard 54 card deck chronicling your journey. In **The Machine** you write a journal about your character's slow descent into madness trying to complete an infernal puzzle in the form of the eponymous contraption. Once your character has perished you pass the journal on to someone else, via post or, if playing completely solo to another 'character' that you have created and they are tasked with creating their own doomed chapter in the story.

If you want your solo rpgs to have more of a balance toward action than story then **Ironsworn** delivers a more traditional tabletop rpg experience in a dark fantasy setting. Played without a GM (although the option is there for full on GM and co-operative mode), you are an Ironsworn taking on quests across a harsh land inspired by Nordic legend. You will engage in combat, roll dice and undertake quests to fulfill vows you have taken. Think of them like end goals, some are easy to complete and others may be longer term quests that may take multiple sessions. The game relies on the player to fill in a lot of the blanks with no GM or set adventures but there are prompts called Oracles which pop up at multiple points in your adventure to keep the story moving.

The best bit about Ironsworn is that it's free. The PDF versions can be downloaded and printed off and, after reading a couple of chapters, you are ready to play. There are expansions available that are chargeable and if you want a nice shiny book you can order one online.

Solo PRG's may lose the social aspect and some of the more interesting or amusing situations that can occur when playing in a group but as a relaxing and at times contemplative experience, there is plenty out there to keep you entertained.

# Dexterity

If you are looking for something that uses a little less tactical thinking, relying instead on physical reflexes and coordination then you don't just have to settle for Jenga. In dexterity games you will be flipping, building and in, **Flick em Up**. yep, you guessed it, flicking your way to victory.

In this WIld West inspired dexterity games, players take turns in flicking their gunslingers into position so that they can be picked off one by one with bullets that you also must flick toward the enemy. It's a fun little game with cardboard buildings to slide into and even wagons and horses to ride. The game comes with scenarios to compete in and as a competitive game it's a neat game with great replayability.

The zombie themed spin off, **Flick em Up: Dead of Winter** works in a cooperative aspect and therefore is suited to solo play. The mechanics are mostly identical with the opportunity to loot buildings for food or supplies but stealth is also worked into the game with knives and baseball bats also available to dispatch your undead foe.

You will want to be as stealthy as possible too as using a gun alerts the horde who will have the opportunity to take you out using their vast numbers. The enemies move is carried out via a dice tower equipped with a trap door roof that you load a number of zombies on to before sending them spilling toward your defenseless hero. It's a great way to simulate the enemy horde attempting to overpower the player and the random result removes any temptation to make things easier on yourself if playing solo.

More flicking can be done in the classic, 150 year old abstract game, **Crokinole**. There is no solo mode here but I would be remiss if I wasn't to mention it when talking about dexterity games. The game takes place on a circular board split into regions along the edge and a circle in the middle. The central circle is marked out with small pegs which players must attempt to flick their disks into, shuffleboard style. If you manage to place your disk into the small hole situated in the centre of this region then you get extra points and feel particularly smug about it. Each round players take turns trying to finish with the most disks closest to the centre by essentially playing a big shiny game of marbles.

The rule that the player going first must flick their disc into the centre and subsequent turns must hit the discs that are already on the board means that no player is ever safe from having their perfectly placed piece pinged off the board to riotous laughter.

Crokinole really is a classic and its simple ruleset means anyone can play. The only issue is the cost. A crokinole board will set you back well over a hundred pounds with many premium boards going way above that so it's probably only worth considering if you know someone who really loves crokinole or if you want a nice circular board with little pegs in it to hang on your wall.

**Flip Ships** is another co-operative game that can be adapted into a solo affair. The clue is in the title as players will flip cardboard tokens (or ships) to try to fight off the alien onslaught trying to conquer earth.

The game works a little like space invaders with alien ships descending in lines from above and it's up to you to utilise your fleet of different ships by flipping them from your base onto the invaders cards. Different ships have different powers allowing them to attack cards on different rows and for the finale you will attempt to flip your ships into the aliens mothership at the top of the table, a tricky prospect to be sure.

Flip ships really nails the space invaders aesthetic and it's such a simple concept executed in a way that makes solo play feel like you are standing at the cabinet in a sticky old arcade fending off the relentless alien hordes.

# Go on then, tell me about the best solo games please!

So far I have tried to avoid passing too much judgment on my favourite games but It's time to share some of the best times I have had so far with solo gaming. While there are some honourable mentions to be made outside of this list (mostly roll and writes that fill those quiet moments at home or in a pub with a quick pint and a small box game in your bag) these are the games that, to date, I've spent the most time with.

And I will start with the biggest of them all, the legacy dungeon crawler mentioned that I mentioned earlier, the absolutely epic Gloomhaven.

## Gloomhaven

One of the first, serious games that I bought as it was top of pretty much everybody's list when it came to solo games. The box weighs in at just under 10 kilogrammes and I was so impressed that I must have asked at least 5 people to pick it up, proudly nodding in silence at their surprised expressions when they felt how chunky this thing was. I actually still offer visitors a 'cheeky lift' of the Gloomhaven box now if it catches their eye as they look over my collection.

And the weight of the box isn't the only impressively daunting aspect of GH. Once all the bits of cardboard have been punched and sorted into bags or boxes you have, what can initially be an overwhelming amount of content to work with.

I will start with the map. It's an impressive beast measuring at 56 x 56cm and printed on thick 'board game' board. It unfolds to depict the titular town of Gloomhaven, where a handful of its missions take place, as well as its surrounding swamps, forests, deserts and mountain ranges. Throughout the campaign you will unlock more and more missions and will place stickers on the numbered locations around the map giving the player a real sense of its scale as you visit sunken ships, haunted woods and icy mountain passes. It's also, in a real sense, completely pointless, the map serves no real purpose for the game, you can just turn to the page with the next mission and work through the game from there. However, as an ingredient in the GH soup, it's the croutons or maybe even the basil leaf you take out before eating. Its sole purpose is to add to the 'videogame' nature of GH.

In fact, GH is the nearest thing to a videogame I have played on my dining table, everything from unlockable characters, each with their own personal goal that, once completed, retires that character, passing on their experiences to its successors. It's in the card based combat that replaces dice rolls with card flips that can add or subtract damage dealt. It's in a campaign in which decisions made at the end of one scenario can completely lock out some missions or storylines, where the loot you find in chests is all laid out in a special table that, if you don't pick it up, could be lost forever.

And.. It's also terrible to lose…. Most of the time

I have two separate GH experiences. One is a co-operative experience with a couple of friends who have their own characters (probably about 5% of my playtime with GH). The other is my solo experience.

The co-operative experience is…..fine, and I'm sure that there are groups of people who have managed to successfully make the time to power through the massive campaign together and had a great experience. I actually enjoyed every game of GH I played with friends, even those that we failed, either due to running out of the action cards you need to take turns or by being murdered by monsters. We would generally just get back on with it, starting again, learning from our mistakes in the hope for better luck next time.

My solo experience is a little less relaxed and to explain why, I need to give an overview of the setup involved and why I maybe wouldn't recommend Gloomhaven for everyone.

So setup involves, firstly finding out which campaign mission you are playing next, this is where the map does actually come in handy, look for a location you have stuck on there and choose one you haven't ticked off yet. There can be issues here if you want to follow a particular story thread as some (a lot) of the missions are 'side missions' that you unlock (very videogame) that might not drive the story on as much as you would like.

Next you find the scenario and build the map. Each scenario's map makes use of GH's many double sided map tiles that slot together to make the dungeon, cave or swampland you will be fighting through. Each map tile has its own label which is listed in the scenario setup along with all of the monsters, traps, doorways, treasure chests and set decorations you will need.

Now if you haven't got yourself a fancy storage system for the ton of cardboard that you now own then you are going to, at a rough guess, take about 40 minutes minimum to set up one scenario. I have cobbled together my own solution using a plastic piano storage case for tokens and a concertina file for map tiles but I still take around 20 minutes to set up before I even start with getting my character deck ready. All in all it's about half an hour from opening the box to starting to play.

Which makes defeat a bitter pill to swallow. It also adds to the delicious tension felt when playing GH as well as the sense of achievement when things work perfectly. It does, however, make a small amount of cheating justified. You see, Gloomhaven, for me anyway, has become less of a board game that I want to beat and more of a story that I am working through, one where failure could happen but only if it serves the narrative I am invested in.

Because Gloomhaven isn't about high scores, it's about being part of an epic fantasy tale. Its characters aren't particularly well fleshed out, its setting not particularly fresh but it is a playset in which you can tell your own story. A playset where I purposefully picked my own Cragheart characters personal quest (something you are supposed to be doing randomly) so that it fitted the backstory I had created. Where I meticulously planned the amount of missions it would take so that my character retired at a point in the campaign where it made sense to me. That was just as satisfying as clutching a win at the last moment in a scenario which seemed doomed to fail. And the perfect thing is you can have both.

So Gloomhaven isn't about high scores, for me, Gloomhaven is about playing a game like dungeons and dragons, on my own because I can, and it's also about having fun in failure with friends if you want to have it both ways, which I do.

Gloomhaven, also, isnt the newest or biggest kid on the block anymore. It now has an even heftier sequel, Frosthaven.

Frosthaven does pretty much the same as its younger sibling and then adds some. Not only is its box bigger but it adds crafting mechanics and buildings that can be built or upgraded in your town. It also streamlines existing stuff where it can. The inbuilt organiser is miles better than Gloomahavens, with only the map tiles and monster tokens requiring you to play a bit of box tetris when packing away. This means that setup is simplified somewhat (a new mechanic requires you to only have to place the first map tile down before starting) so solo sessions can a little less of a chore.

My only issue with Frosthaven is that, despite it sitting just out of my eyeline as I write this, I haven't got it to the table yet. This is simply because Gloomhaven is such a massive game and a time commitment that I haven't managed to finish its campaign yet.

This begs the question, do you need them both? And if not, which one do you buy?

If you are on the fence and don't feel like committing you could go for neither.

Gloomhaven: Jaws of the Lion, is a smaller spin off with less characters, less missions and less faff. It's also considerably cheaper. To Set up the map you simply open the mission book to the relevant page and there it is for you to play on. It's a simple solution to one of the biggest issues I have with Gloomhaven and the game itself acts as a great introduction to the series. It does lack the bombastic scope of its bigger cousins so the choice is yours whether you just jump straight in with the bigger box versions.

## Sprawlopolis

From the biggest box I own to the smallest, Sprawlopolis is a 'wallet game' that actually comes in a small wallet you can fit in your back pocket.

Sprawlopolis' entire game takes place across its 18 cards and can be played on an ironing board! Each card is split into 4 quarters, each depicting a different 'districsts' that can be identified easily by their colour - commercial, industrial, parks and residential areas. Each card also features at least one road that runs through at least one of these areas.

The game is simple, draw a hand of 3 cards and start placing them down to build your city, adding a card from the 15 card deck (not 18, more on that later) after you play each card. You can overlap areas as long as certain simple rules are followed and, once finished you score your city.

For each of the 4 colour coded areas you score 1 point per block in the largest group of each area. You then subtract 1 point for each road in your city. A road is a continuous stretch of highway so if you have managed to piece together all of your roads in one continuous line then you are very clever and probably cheating, nonetheless you will only deduct 1 point.

That's not it though, Sprawlopolis has a variable scoring system. Remember I said the game takes place using 18 cards but you have a deck of 15? That's because, before you start playing you draw 3 cards and turn them face down revealing (shock, horror!) that each card has a different scoring condition on its reverse side. These are the bonus scoring conditions that will bag you the big points. They are also the cards that will define the score limit you have to hit to win!

Each scoring card is numbered 1 - 18 and when you draw the 3 cards you add up each scoring condition to make your target. These cards not only net you points but can also lose you points if you fail to fulfill its condition

As an example, card number 15 gives you 2 points for each orange residential block adjacent to 2 or more grey industrial blocks. This means that if you pulled this card along with Card number 1 (which gives you points for every road that ends inside your city but takes away a point for every road that ends at the edge of the city by the way) then your scoring condition would be 16. If your third scoring condition card was 14 (1 point for every road section that is in a completed loop, of course!) then your scoring goal would be 30 points.

Once you have added your largest zones, taken away your roads then added or subtracted all of your scoring condition cards then you have your final score. It's likely going to be less than your target because this game is super tough. But it's also super short and so simple to start again with the same conditions or shuffle a different set of score cards.

And that's Sprawlopolis, you can buy some pretty cheap, one card expansions that add a few new mechanics but they aren't necessary.

So why is this game one of my favourite solo titles? The simplicity is a massive part of it, it's a game you will be playing within minutes with only a couple of checks in the tight little rulebook to keep you on track. You will also be playing your second, third or fourth game (you absolute madman) in no time. The game's 10 minute playtime means that my inevitable and certain failure isn't a bad thing. It's part of the game. The variable scoring condition isn't really a target to hit for me, it's a way to explore the games many intricate scoring mechanics to see how I can plan having orange zones on the edge of my city while still having them surrounded by grey zones but all the while ensuring blue zones are nowhere near, or that my roads all connect. Quite often the scoring combinations seem impossible, some actually might be, but through constant play and a deck that shuffles itself naturally when you put it back in the box, you are always learning everytime you take it for a spin. It's the closest 'solitaire' game to solitaire in my collection and I would argue that it's better than the one Napoleon hammered back in the day.

The games theme doesn't need to lift the gameplay but, if you need it to be thematic then the city building is all in there, albeit in a weird way with roads that go nowhere and housing estates next to smoke belching factories and shopping centres.

Another word on that scoring, yes you are encouraged to randomly pick 3 cards to play as your scoring condition cards each game but what I have done now I have played it so much is compiled a 'greatest hits' collection of conditions, one that grows each time I play. If I happen to draw 3 particularly dicey score cards, I won't just reshuffle after failure, I will replay under the same conditions, looking for ways to manipulate this tiny deck (and there are many ways that will become apparent after a few playthroughs) to get close to that goal. This is all despite the fact that the goal doesn't really matter, well at least not until you are so good at it that you can consistently get close. I am not at that level.

Sprawlopolis is the kind of game where I could get to that level though, one day. Just by having it in my pocket (or wallet) when I'm out affords me opportunities for a quick game or three. These are games where I won't necessarily be studying it but where I will be absorbing new techniques through some form of osmosis. It's my 'phone game' one I can play while watching television if I have a flat surface around (like an ironing board) and eventually it will sink in and I'll be like when your grandparents have played Candy Crush so much that they can clear a screen in 4 moves.

## Marvel Champions

I own a number of LCG's. All are card games that demand further investment beyond the initial purchase of their starter sets to get the most out of them. And while Arkham Horror: The Card Game is arguably the better that I own and even though The Lord of The Rings: The Card Game manages to weave a rich narrative and challenge, Marvel Champions is the one that I have invested more time and a whole lot more money into.

It's most likely the theme, which does a lot of the heavy lifting and it's likely that if you aren't a Marvel fan then it all may fall a bit flat. The more that I get into Marvel Champions though, the more I play around with its numerous decks and new mechanics (all through extra purchases of course) the more I start thinking about it when I'm not playing it. In fact, it's probably the only game I have played the most during the writing of this book and, without blowing the solo bubble too much, it's the only game myself and a fellow boardgamer have played together for months on the rare occasions we get together.

In Marvel Champions, each player controls a hero, in solo you can play with two heroes or go fully solo single hero, the game's difficulty is well designed to scale this way. Your objective is to defeat the villain by reducing his hit points to zero in two stages, the second of which he will grow stronger. You need to do this before he either reduces your hit points to zero or completes his main scheme by placing a predetermined number of scheme counters on it.

Your hero is a deck of cards, the first of which is double sided displaying the hero itself, Spiderman, Iron Man Black Panther etc.. and the other side showing their alter ego. A chunk of the deck is made up of a series of cards specific to that character that can be used to inflict damage on the villain or stop them from scheming and is usually themed around the hero's powers. The majority of the deck is made up of one of 4 different 'aspects'. These aspects are, Justice, leadership, Aggression and Protection which are all built around a certain style of play. Finally there are some basic cards in every deck that do fairly generic, if essential actions.

On your turn you can flip your character card once to your hero or alter ego side. The key is you can only attack (or be attacked) or thwart the villains scheme as your hero and you generally can only rest and heal as your alter ego, the kicker being that, in this mode, the villain will scheme while you are in alter ego form, adding more tokens on that evil plan that will eventually end the game.

So it's a balance of building up combinations of attacks or thwart actions and unleashing them as a hero before backing out quickly to heal and regroup. All the while dealing with villain cards that can pile on the pressure through extra attacks, extra side schemes that can force you to deal with them before concentrating on the main scheme, ramping up extra tokens on the main scheme, accelerating your defeat.

Each card you play has a cost associated with it, a cost that has to be paid by using other cards in your hand. This forces a delicate balancing act leaving you constantly looking at your hand agonising over a play you want to make that requires you to sacrifice a card you may need further down the line. Soon enough though you will have a table full of upgrades, reaction cards and sidekicks that you can activate each turn, putting the hurt on the villain as you whittle down his health to zero just in time.

And therein lies one of the main criticisms of Marvel Champions. It's a game where you butt heads with the baddie until one of you falls. Whereas Arkham Horror has quickly (over its many many expansions) built in new mechanics and more interesting win conditions, Marvel Champions hasn't changed a whole lot and, in a criticism I can't help but kind of share, you quite often know you are going to win a few turns in advance so the thrill of victory can be dampened more often than not with a shrug.

In all fairness, the game hasn't been out as long as it's Eldritch themed cousin and now has a number of big box expansions that contain campaigns where you can go up against the likes of Red Skull, take on bad guys from The Guardians of the Galaxy and even Fight Thanos and his Black Order. Each of these campaigns has layered on a few more mechanics and a legacy type mode where cards can be removed or added to your deck based on events in precious battles. As a Marvel fan, the future looks good for the title if they can carry on coming up with new ideas to keep the gameplay fresh.

A lot of the current freshness comes from the new character decks though. Outside of the 5 you get with the main starter pack you get 2 new heroes with each big box expansion. Single hero packs are also available and regularly released. Each of these does interesting things with the game. Ant-Man for example comes with a folded hero card. On one side is Scott Lang (the alter ego), the other has tiny little ant man, unfold it and you get the giant version of ant man with his own special powers. Ant-Mans deck is all about flipping between each state, with cards that allow you to do this more than the usual once per turn inflicting damage, thwarting or healing depending on which state you are in. Dr Strange's hero deck comes with its own separate 'invocation' deck that you can use to bend the games rules in devastating ways. It's a totally different way to play the game and really leans into the theme of the character.

There are so many heroes to buy and play with that the game stays fresh and fun just experimenting with ways to enjoy it. I've already poured far too much into buying new decks and I havent got half those that I want or played enough with those that I have.

While the campaign part of the game is something I have enjoyed mainly with a friend. I have still played more of the game solo. This is mostly experimenting with new heroes, adding a different aspect to the deck and taking on a new villain one on one, adjusting the very flexible difficulty by adding new cards to their deck or by adjusting the amount of damage they do. One of the villain expansions, The Green Goblin, even comes with its own alter ego for the villain himself and two full scenario decks to work through.

It's through playing these solo games that I learn more about the hero decks, how to use the ever expanding number of cards to create synergies or new tactics to take on bigger, stronger villains. The game can be punishing with a level of swinging randomness that can kill you quickly if you are unlucky. Fortunately, tear down is fairly quick and with a semi well thought out storage system (a printer and some cardboard partitions are your friend or you can go to Etsy for a fancy storage box or 6) I can be swapping out new cards fairly quickly and getting back on with the fight.

I wouldn't say Marvel Champions is the best solo game that I own, it's a big, dumb money pit that takes up a load of table space but it's one that I can sit with on an afternoon, with a cuppa or a beer, some music on or watching TV and just pick through, turning over encounter cards and groaning at my awful luck or punching the air when I put together an awesome combo that makes me look like a massive genius rather than a big dumb kid playing with his superhero cards.

## Eldritch Horror

Eldritch Horror is a big, heavy  box of cardboard that takes players on a globetrotting journey battling lovecraftian horrors, their minions and the cultists who love them.

On your turn you will rush between locations, criss-crossing the globe in an attempt to close gates to other worlds, battle hordes of monsters and eventually solve mysteries to defeat the big bad and save the day.

Along the way you will be playing cooperatively (perfect for solo) against the game. The problem is, the game does not like to play fair.

Each action you take usually requires a 'check' that involves rolling a number of D6 based on your character's stats. Succeed in this check and you move one step towards success but failure can be devastating at pretty much any point in the game. The results of your check can be manipulated by using a number of modifiers based on equipment you may start with from the in-game shop. These weapons, spells or items can help balance the increasingly long odds in your favour as you strike the balance between racing against time to end the supernatural threat and ensuring your flimsy investigators are prepared to face horrors from other realms.

Things can quickly turn from bad to 'ohmygoditisover' very quickly as you not only have to contend with an Omen tracker that is constantly counting down to doom. But the 'Mythos' phase that occurs once you have taken all of your actions each round. When you have taken your turn to move around the board, pick up items and prepare, players have to perform an action based on the space they ended up on. These actions can help you toward your goal of harvesting clues to be victorious or can be combat encounters seeing you face off against monsters on the board, either to thin out the herd or simply so that you can escape to the relative safety of an empty space and resume your investigation. After this, the Mythos phase heaps more misery on players by spawning more monster spewing gates, filling the board with more adversaries, advancing the Omen Tracker or placing rumor tokens on the board that will initiate short, side quests that need to be dealt with quickly before they snowball into game ending events. Every now and again the Mythos phase can throw something nice into the mix but, as the game goes on, these instances become increasingly rare.

Eldritch Horror isn't the most relaxing solo game on this list but it drips with atmosphere and its many expansions add extra mechanics that keep the game fresh for multiple playthroughs.

It would be stretch to describe a solo session of the game as a puzzle, sure it requires careful planning and strategy but the game can quickly throw enough at you that sometimes it's just stacked against you in a way that you can't win.

These are fairly rare occasions though, and you would be pretty unlucky to suffer repeated games of Eldritch Horror where this happens. I have never found myself packing the game away, even when I have lost, overly disappointed with the experience, even if I have felt the outcome was unfair.

## Elder Sign

The owner of my friendly local game shop described Elder Sign as Cthulhu Yahtzee, which isn't the worst way to sum it up. Again we are in the realm of Eldritch, Lovecraftian horror which is probably the perfect theme suited to solo play due to the nature of being up against often insurmountable odds.

This time though you have dice, lots of dice, to overcome those odds.

Elder Sign places players amongst the curios and occult artifacts of a 1920's museum. A place where the barriers between our world and the realm beyond have begun to leak open unleashing fierce creatures heralding the arrival of a destructive ancient one.

Investigators are tasked with attempting to stave off the arrival of the ancient one by collecting 'Elder Signs', once a certain number of signs are collected, the evil is sealed away, if investigators fail to do this within a certain time then they must defeat the unleashed ancient creature or its game over.

To do all of this is very simple, you pick a location to visit from one of the 6 or more cards on the table and roll your dice. Each die has a number of symbols on each face, scrolls, magnifying glass, skull or ominous tentacles (usually bad) some of the symbols may have a number on them such as, three magnifying glasses. Each location card will have a number of corresponding symbols on it that must be covered with a die before the location is 'completed'

For example, a card may have a very large nasty on it along with a '2 skull' symbol and a scroll with a 3 next to it. If you rolled your 6 green dice and were lucky enough to roll 2 skulls and either a scroll with a 3 next to it or 3 single scrolls you could 'complete' that card, beat the baddie and claim the prizes that come with said card. If one of these prizes is an Elder sign then you are one step closer to victory.

If you didn't manage to get exactly what you wanted you can take the opportunity to re-roll but have to use one less die for each subsequent roll. You could have, for example, only rolled one skull with the rest of your die showing symbols that are no good to you, in this case you can place the skull on the card and roll the rest of your die (minus one for the re-roll)

Along with Elder signs you can gain clue tokens that give you free re-rolls or items that you can use to grant you access to special, yellow and red dice that increase your odds of a favorable outcome. Each card has different rewards at the bottom so you can pick which you want to tackle, unsurprisingly those with the greatest rewards are often the most difficult to beat.

If you fail to cover all of the symbols before running out of dice rolls however, then you will suffer the penalty denoted at the bottom of the car. Penalties can come in the form of physical or horror damage, doom tokens that will speed up the arrival of the ancient one or monsters that are added to cards to increase their difficulty (but can also offer their own rewards).

Turns are made up of moving your investigator to a location and resolving the card through the dice rolls, you can also choose to take refuge in the museum lobby where you can take the opportunity to regain some of your health or sanity (yep…!) or spend accumulated in-game currency to buy items, extra dice rolls or even elder signs themselves.

While all this is happening though, the clock is ticking. After each players turn you move the in-game clocks hands forward. Each time it hits midnight (every 4 turns) a card is revealed that will throw some spanner in the works so it's best not to dilly dally too much, not least because if the ancient one is eventually released it's very difficult to overcome them without a lot of preparation and a boat load of luck.

If you do manage to get the required amount of Elder signs then that's it, the game just kind of ends which is probably a little anticlimactic for some. I would also say that,even though the cards have small snippets of flavour text to enhance the theme, more often than not this text gets ignored, literally changing the game to yahtzee with monsters.

But that's not necessarily a bad thing, if you want globetrotting adventures or dungeon crawling epic encounters then you can play Eldritch Horror, Gloomhaven or Mansions of Madness. If you want a casual dice tosser that is quick to set up and requires a minimal amount of strategy and theme that's there if you look for it then I would point you toward Elder Sign, its relatively inexpensive in it's base format and has some cheap expansions that really add a lot to the game  such as new dice mechanics and locations should you feel the desire to explore further.

## One Deck Dungeon

Most solo games are hard. A lot of them are designed this way to make up for the lack of engagement that comes from playing solo. If it was easy then I guess there would be little point to playing.

One Deck Dungeon is one of the hard games, sometimes it's

unfair, a lot of the times it seems impossible but it comes in a little box, is filled with lovely dice to roll and it's quick and easy to set up. If the theme of Elder Sign put you off or if you wanted something that had a bit more meat to it (at least on the surface) then this could be the game for you.

Players take control of 4 adventurers taken from the usual fantasy archetypes, Ranger, Rogue, Mage or Barbarian and have to work their way down through a dungeon before facing off against the boss.

During their quest through the dungeon, these characters can level up using XP from monsters, gain items that add extra dice rolls to their character or spells that can be activated to mitigate damage, alter dice rolls etc.

The dungeon in One Deck Dungeon, is a deck of cards. Each card has a door on its back and either a trap or monster on its reverse side. Adventurers will have to work through this deck to the bottom where they will reach the stairs to take them down to the next level. At this point they shuffle the deck and start again. This is done 3 times, with each level adding extra challenges that need to be overcome before facing the boss.

Turns start with the player discarding 2 cards from the top of the deck, signifying the passage of time. This will become important because as time passes, so too do opportunities to get stronger and prepare for a tough final battle. After this there are 2 choices, firstly you must 'explore' by drawing up to 4 cards and placing them door side up, these are the 4 doors that house your first opponents. The second option is to open one of these doors. On each turn you can only take one action so if you explore on one turn you must discard another 2 cards before opening a door.

Once a door is opened you flip your chosen card and see what is in store, you then have the option to fight it or run away with no penalty other than that being the end of your turn. The other option is to fight, and it's something you will need to do a lot of if you want to get stronger.

There are 3 different coloured dice you will use to fight in One Deck Dungeon. The yellow die is for strength challenges, pink is for dexterity and blue is for magic. There is also a 4th, black die that is 'wild' and can be used as any colour you wish if you have it.

Your choice of starting character will dictate how any of these die you get to roll in combat. A mage would roll 4 blue magic dice but only one yellow strength die for example.

Each monster card has a number of coloured spaces that you must try to cover with your dice or suffer the consequences. These spaces correspond to the 3 different coloured dice that you will roll and will have a value that you must equal or beat with the correct coloured die to cover. Alongside this, each encounter requires you to also cover a space on a card that signifies which level of the dungeon you are on. This will heap additional misery on you if left uncovered at the end of the encounter so it's wise to sacrifice one of your rolls to do so. If you manage to cover all of the spaces on the card with the correct combination of die then you come away scott free and take the card as your prize.

If you fail then each uncovered space will come with a penalty. This will either be a time penalty that forces you to discard even more cards and opportunities from your deck, or a damage penalty that will take a number of hearts from your small health pool. Once this pool is depleted, it's game over.

You can use some neat tricks to cover these spaces though, abilities or spells can be activated to change your results or you can combine dice you don't need and transform them into wild dice to cover spaces. The only caveat here is that the wild dice can only be the same value as the lowest of the two you are combining so it's not always useful.

Regardless of whether you filled every space, as long as you're not dead then you get to claim the monster card. Each card has different symbols on 3 of its edges and, once claims you can use it in 3 different ways

One side of the card can be used as an item to improve your stats and increase your dice rolls or your health. For example, you could defeat a monster that gives you an extra 2 yellow strength rolls each turn or an extra magic roll and one more health point.

The second thing you can do is use the monster for its 'XP'. This value is shown by a number of small flames at the top of the card. Once you hit a certain threshold of XP you can level up your character. This is an essential step in getting through the game as it allows you to hold more items and therefore have more dice to roll, it also gives you access to more potions that can replenish your health as well as allow you to learn more skills.

Skills are the third thing you can use your defeated enemies for. As you come across stronger enemies, their skill rewards can improve your choices when it comes to finding ways to manipulate those rolls.

As you might have guessed, the fact that each defeated monster can only be used in one of these ways can provide the player with some dilemmas but also gives the game a lot more depth when it comes to building a character that is able to make its way through the dungeon safely. When it comes to that final battle, the choices you have made can really mount up which is one of the greatest but most frustrating things about the game.

On one hand it's very satisfying to build your character into a seemingly unstoppable force, sometimes it may feel wiser to have a more rounded out set of dice rolls with an even number of coloured dice at your disposal. Other times you may want to focus on one particular colour in the hope that you pull out adversaires that suit your style.

And sometimes you will pick a skill that looks great on paper but you just don't get a chance to use because you draw cards that don't play into your tactics. One other thing that kind of unravels the tactical nature of character building is one that you can't really escape, and that is the fact that higher rolls are always better. It's rare that you will celebrate a 1 or a 2, in fact a lot of the monsters will have skills that can mitigate these rolls entirely, adding insult to injury.

One Deck Dungeon does have a place in my collection and my heart though and that's partly because of its miniature campaign mode. Once you choose a character you can run the gauntlet over and over again hitting milestones that enable you to buff certain aspects of their stats or add extra dice rolls as you take on harder difficulty settings and more complex dungeons and bosses. I'm clearly a fan of the game, as well as its sci fi themed sequel, One Deck Galaxy.

Paul Oyston

# That is a lot of games, where on Earth do I start?

### Digital Adaptations

So you know some of the genres and a small selection of the titles available but with constant new releases and an already huge library of games on offer, deciding where to start is really tough. Board games aren't the cheapest investment and while there are some smaller games with reasonable price tags it can be daunting to make a purchase based on guesswork or reviews. Sometimes you need to be able to get in there and test the waters with minimum risk.

There are a load more digital adaptations of tabletop games

becoming available on PC, console and mobile that usually offer the opportunity for online play as well as solo games against the A.I.

Games such as Root, Agricola, Scythe and Wingspan are all cheaper options than their physical editions that will give you a great idea of whether you would want to take the leap. In some cases these editions may be all you need for your solo ventures, I have spent a lot of time playing the digital edition of the deck building game, Splendor, almost to the point where buying it physically would just be so that I could own a set of the satisfyingly hefty poker style chips that come with it.

If playing against A.I isn't for you but you still want to stick to digital then there are a few virtual tabletop options such as Tabletopia, Board Game Arena and Tabletop Simulator where you can pick up and roll dice, shuffle decks of cards and move meeples and components.

The advantage of a programme such as Tabletop Simulator is that, once you have purchased it, you can try pretty much any game out there for free via fan made mods or for a small charge via official versions. The downside is that it can be quite clunky, with games that should take less than an hour stretching out to fill entire evenings as you struggle with the interface. Accidentally picking up the entire deck instead of the top card without realising is a common occurrence even after hours of play.

There is also the ethical question around using fan made content with no contribution being given to the developer. It's always urged that, should you enjoy trying the game on Tabletop Simulator, that you should seek out buying a physical copy where possible. Personally I have found some of my favourite games such as Cosmic Encounter, playing Tabletop Simulator. As soon as a copy became available I snapped it up, unfortunately, getting the perfect amount of players to a real life table isn't always easy but I know that the digital version is there if I need to get a fix. Some developers actively encourage users to add mods of their titles to the platform as it can drum up interest in people buying physical copies further down the road and there are some chargeable, official mods available made by the creators of the games.

As a risk free way of seeing what's out there, I would thoroughly recommend using one of these services and with more and more developers using them as a way to get their products in front of gamers, there will likely be more opportunities to find official reproductions in the future. Premium subscriptions are available for both Boardgame Arena and Tabletopia so if you want to ensure support is given to the creators, then the option is there.

## BGG

If the cost factor of buying a pc or laptop to play board games puts you off and the idea of squinting at your phone gives you a migraine then let's see how to turn some of those physical games into solo experiences.

It's probably about time I mentioned BoardGameGeek (BGG).

Founded in 2000 BGG is a database that has grown to be the

place to go for everything tabletop. It is filled with reviews, forums and resources on pretty much every game out there. It's a community that shares ideas for new games, one that creators and publishers regularly interact with and one where you always find out if a game is playable solo.

Within each game's forums you will usually find a thread that discusses a solo mode. Sometimes these are homebrew versions, put together by players in their spare time, testing how they can manipulate game mechanics to work for one player. Other times they are team efforts or put together by experienced or up and coming game developers who want to try their hand at tinkering around with the rulesets. The great thing is they are all free, and because of the nature of an internet forum, feedback can be left and discussions can be had around what worked and what didn't. This can result in real collaborative, community efforts that can yield impressive results.

I want to talk about Root (again) and specifically its official solo mode. Root's first expansion included two new factions and was also bundled with an automated version of the Marquis De Cat, dubbed 'the Mechanical Marquis'. Soon after its release, a growing number within the BGG community of players found this automa too much of a push over. It didn't take long until a fan made project began. Benjamin Schmauss', The Better Bot Project, sought to improve the existing automa and went further by creating similar, automated versions for all 4 of the base factions. This initiative was so successful that the publisher, Leder Games incorporated it into an official release, The Clockwork Expansion, that includes full boards for the 4 factions (including, The Mechanical Marquis 2.0). This version makes Root into not only a fantastic solo experience but it changes the game for smaller groups who are now able to play the game as intended with a full complement of factions with the automa filling in the missing slots.

## DIY

What should you do if you haven't got a community of super boffins churning out new and exciting solo variants? What if the game has just come out? Maybe it's time you got in there yourself and created your own solo rules!

The first step would be to look at what is an essential element of the multiplayer game that cannot be taken away (without ruining the experience). The best way to do this is to play the game in a multiplayer situation. Now if you could do this then you probably wouldn't need a solo mode right? Okay so, play it in a multiplayer situation by playing as each player. Now I know that I said way back at the beginning of this book that solo play isn't about shuffling around a table pretending to be 3 or 4 different players but, by doing this you will uncover what makes the game tick and, essentially, what can be sacrificed for solo play.

Ask yourself, does your opponent need to have a hidden hand of cards to choose from or would it be just as simple on their turn to draw the top card from the deck and play it for that action? What if they have a choice of actions? Is it maybe better to put together a list of those actions in order of importance so that, in a situation where your opponent can take an action that would score them a victory point or gain an advantage that they do this.

Maybe if they are unable to do this for whatever reason (they may lack the required resource or be in the wrong place on the board) that they instead do the 'next best thing'. The key is to create an opponent that isn't just blocking or antagonising you as a player but instead follows some form of logical rules. If an element of randomisation or luck can be implemented then that can transform a solo experience from a more puzzle based experience into something a little more natural.

Not that there's anything wrong with a puzzle element to solitaire games. The roll and write game, Cartographers has very little player interaction. It's a roll and write game where you are enlisted to map out terrain in a magical kingdom. Instead of rolling dice you flip the top card from a deck and have to draw the results on your sheet. The interaction comes when you draw a monster card. When this happens you are supposed to pass your sheet to an opposition player who then decides where to place an obstacle that would cause you the biggest problem. This is translated to the solo mode in the form of a small icon on the monster card that symbolises which corner of your pad you should place the obstacle if nobody is there to do it on your behalf.

It's best to simplify what should happen when it comes to direct interaction between players in a solo mode. Sometimes you may eliminate any form of aggression by an automa unless it's a last resort. You may even take away entire elements of the automas turn, for example, in the solo mode for Viticulture, the automa doesn't actually build on their own player board, they don't harvest or crush grapes or blend and store wines in their cellar. Instead the game makes some assumptions that this is happening and instead makes you deal with the actions that occur either side of this element, such as placing workers and the resulting points achieved from selling wines.

The key to take away from this is that the 'player board' element isn't important in solo mode. If you have no control or interaction with it in a multiplayer game then why would you want to do so in a solo mode. The heart of the game is working against what goes in and what comes out of your opponents vineyard, not what happens there. To put it another way, do you really want to be messing about placing grapes in crush pads and juggling cards for another player when you have your own game to play? To have to do this would extend the game massively and ultimately, be a bit of a drag. Viticulture solo mode concentrates on the things that directly affect you, such as the opponent stopping you from placing workers where you want to and by the opponent scoring points.

Once you have started working on a solo mode, ask someone to play it for you. Take feedback, play it yourself until you break it. Hopefully along the way you will find the one key element that brings it together. It certainly won't be perfect but as you do it more it will get better.

There are tons of resources available though and BGG is the perfect place to find tips and even share your own solo mode ideas and gain valuable feedback. The best thing about solo gaming is that it is only growing bigger so if you want to work out a way to play your newest purchase on your own then you can guarantee someone else is having the same idea over on BGG.

## Budget Options

Whether you already have a pile of games that sit unplayed due to your lack of humans to play with or if you fancy diving straight into the solo gaming sphere then it may be puzzling where to start.

My first solo purchases were Gloomhaven and Arkham Horror: The Card Game and both are widely recognised as two of the best solo experiences available. However, Gloomhaven and its sequel, Frosthaven are both pricey fellas and Arkham Horror is a bottomless well of investment if it gets its hooks into you. While I certainly wouldn't warn you away from either of these games it may be more worthwhile to dip your toes in gently before committing a mortgage payment to the hobby.

You can't go wrong with a copy of Railroad Ink in any of its formats for less than the price of a couple of cinema tickets. With that you will have one of the best roll and writes available. In all honesty, most roll and writes are priced reasonably due to their general lack of pricey components so, Welcome To, Cartographers or Ganz Schon Clever (That's Pretty Clever) are all reasonably priced, risk free ways to start your solo collection.

Pocket sized Sprawlopolis and a number of the wallet games from Button Shy such as Circle the Wagons and Ragemore are all light on your finances and your shelf (!!). There is a constant stream of new titles being released on a monthly basis from the publisher and the brilliant thing about Button Shy games, other than the price and great design, is the variation on offer with each new game.

The Oniverse series are all games built for solo play so are a great way to dip your toe in, Onirim is a neat little car drafting/hand management card game and Sylvion uses similar mechanics mixed with strategy and tower defense, I have already mentioned Nautilion but any of the games in this series are a good place to start, they all come in smaller boxes and usually include an expansion or two to add longevity.

Speaking of small boxes, the Tiny Epic series is famed for packing a whole load of bits and pieces into their titles, from tiny little pirate ships to 'cute' zombies and even Mechs. While the series is primarily designed for competitive play, most of the titles do have a well thought out solo mode and are easy to pick up and learn for beginners.

# Okay, I'm in. What next?

I am going to assume you have tried and loved all of these little beginner games and want to expand into something meaty and wallet draining. Well here we are, the final showdown, expandable games that you can replay over and over again.

I've already spoken in detail about Marvel Champions as a Living Card Game and it's where I have poured most of my investment so I'm likely biased when I say it gets my recommendation as a solo game you will keep coming back to (and spending money on). There are already a load of 'big' box expansions to the game that have their own set of villains, a couple of new heroes and a small campaign to work through. Individual hero packs can be bought separately, all with pre-built decks that you can swap out with other cards in your collection to customise your play style. There are over 25 of these decks available with a steady stream of new heroes and campaign expansions planned.

The Marvel LCG pales in comparison in terms of card count when compared to the expansions available for Arkham Horror: The Card Game. In addition to its core box set there are currently 7 campaign expansions that comprise of its own core box and 6 additional 'mythos packs' that complete the story. Fortunately, Fantasy Flight have recently begun re-releasing these individual expansions in one complete box meaning that new players can experience a full campaign without having to hunt down individual packs that may be out of print or are selling for higher prices.

If card games aren't your thing *(and you don't want me to start talking about the Lord of the Rings card game that has a mind boggling amount of*

*expansions and character packs)* then maybe a dungeon crawler with plastic spooks and monsters? Set in a spooky mansion? Something you can use an app to help with setting up, setting the scene and ushering you through its spooky stories? **Mansions of Madness** isn't concerned with the over saturation of H.P Lovecraft themed games, it proudly flaunts its 5 expansions in addition to its chunky base game. There is plenty of variety on offer too with each expansion offering up twists on the core game play.

The app randomises enemy encounters and item locations so you never quite play the same game twice, you've just got to find all the cash and the space to store everything.

And just like the cyclical nature of time I come back round to talking about Gloomhaven! If you have come this far, played all the smaller games, tried a couple of LCG's and have enjoyed their solo narrative experience then it may be time to track down a copy of it or its sequel Frosthaven. There are hours of content crammed into both, so much you will likely not use all of the characters or complete all of the quests on offer due to the vastness of it;s campaign and systems. In the interest of bias though you may find that the epic Mage Knight or **The 7th Continent** weave a better tale for you, both are massively popular with solo gamers and will fill plenty of evenings and rainy weekends.

And finally, for fans of bite size solo experiences who also love 80's slasher films, **Final Girl** is a title with a steady stream of expansions. The game puts players in the shoes of the titular final girl of any famous horror movie who must defeat the slasher to survive. Each expansion outside of the core box comes as its own 'feature film' in a cool, VHS style box with an entirely separate storyline and theme based on classic horror flicks. Currently in its second season, Final Girl continues to receive new content.

## Have Fun!

The journey you go on is up to you but I hope you take the first step and try on a solo game or two. It is genuinely an enriching experience that changed my life at a time when the world seemed to be falling apart and human interaction was at a bare minimum. Tabletop gaming as a whole offers a break from the screen and forces us to slow down and develop a number of cognitive skills, helps with problem solving, decision making and logical thinking so it's a hobby I would encourage anyone to pursue whether they have friends or not.

The titles listed within this book are by no means a definitive list, these are titles I have played myself via recommendation from massive communities in BGG and through various board game discord chat channels. There are fistfuls of games I have left out and so many that I have discovered while writing this book that I could rabbit on about for endless pages so I would recommend you do your research, go to your friendly local game shop, pick up some boxes and ask the staff their opinions, I'm sure they will be delighted you are in there in the first place!

Go to a board game cafe if you are lucky enough to live near one, like the traditional games shops, these places are filled with people who absolutely love to offer their opinion, you never know, you might just find your next favourite game.

Above all

Thanks for reading and happy gaming!

# About the Author

If you have made it all the way to the end of this book then thank you so much, if you have just flipped straight to this page then I had better make a good impression to get you to read it.

I am Paul, I live in the North East of England with 3 pretty decent kids, a selection of Pets and a lovely wife, Kerry. I had to start wearing a cap in my late twenties when I started going bald, The genetics made it inevitable.

I enjoy gaming of all kinds, video, board and mind. When I'm not in the kitchen batch cooking, I am outside pretending to enjoy triathlon. You can often find me swimming in a river, cycling down a lane or plodding up a big hill somewhere in the world. Tales of some of my silly fitness exploits can be found over at www.triguy.co.uk and I can be found on Twitter at @pauloyston come say hello and we can talk about the things we both like.

# Acknowledgments

Thank you to Kerry, my wife, for your love, your belief, support and constant encouragement, I'm sorry it took so long to finish this thing. Thanks to my kids, Louis and Willow for playing some actual games with me when they arrived so I could work out the rules (even though I know half the time you were bored) and to Tyler for asking if I was 'working on the book' every time I sat in front of my laptop *(I usually wasn't but I should have been).*

Thank you to Shelly for creating my cover and your dedication to finding 'nice dice'. To my Brother, Ste who loves the Dude so much and my Mum and Dad for buying me Space Hulk when I was a nipper *(although I reckon that you have either stolen or lost my copy of Bloodbowl, Dad)*

Thanks to Hannah for your help with editing and for being the first proper 'boardgamer' I showed this too, also, thanks for opening and punching your copy of Scythe so that I could get a photo.

A special thanks to the strangers I played Cosmic Encounter

online with during the early months of lockdown 2020, you inspired me to start this book and I still cant get anyone to play that game with me in real life!

*Thanks for reading! Please add a short review on Amazon        and let me know what you thought!*

Printed in Great Britain
by Amazon

23857363R00086